PRAYING THE

BOOK OF ACTS

AND THE GENERAL EPISTLES

PRAYING THE
BOOK OF ACTS

AND THE GENERAL EPISTLES

Elmer L. Towns

Destiny Image® Publishers, Inc.
P.O. Box 310
Shippensburg, PA 17257-0310

*"Speaking to the Purposes of God for this Generation
and for the Generations to Come."*

For Worldwide Distribution, Printed in the U.S.A.

ISBN 13: 978-0-7684-2349-3

This book and all other Destiny Image, Revival Press, MercyPlace, Fresh Bread, Destiny Image Fiction, and Treasure House books are available at Christian bookstores and distributors worldwide.

1 2 3 4 5 6 7 8 9 10 11 / 09 08 07

For a U.S. bookstore nearest you, call
1-800-722-6774.

For more information on foreign distributors, call
717-532-3040.

Or reach us on the Internet:
www.destinyimage.com

DEDICATION

It's only natural that a book on *Praying* should be dedicated to praying people. When I began teaching the Pastor's Bible Class (attendance 1,400) at my church in 1978, I also joined the early morning prayer meeting held there.

I bless these people who have done more to bless my ministry than any other group. I've often said, "This is my most important meeting of each week. I wouldn't miss it because I get so much from it." Why? Because with prayer the weak can become strong.

The book by C. Peter Wagner, *Prayer Shield*, challenged me to get prayer partners for my ministry. So I read parts of that book to the early Sunday morning prayer meeting. Then I asked these prayer warriors a question that seemed selfish because it was about the things I was doing. I asked them, *"Will you make my ministry your ministry of prayer?"* Then I continued, asking them, "Don't make a spur of the moment decision, pray about it for a week. Make sure it's of God."

A week later Buddy Bryant said God was putting that burden upon his heart. We've prayed together ever since. Therefore, I dedicate this book, *Praying the Book of Acts and the General Epistles*, to him and the team of intercessors: Priscilla Baker, Margie Balta, Katie Bowles, Buddy Bryant, Harry and Janet Coric, Randy Dodge, Tip and Laurie Killingsworth, Trudy LaMar, Don May, Martin and Edwina Morgan, Esther Morrison, Linda Norris, Charlie Padgett, Faye Wilson, and Charles Yancey.

TABLE OF CONTENTS

Book of Acts

PRAYING THE BOOK OF ACTS
1:1–28:31

THE STORY OF WRITING THE BOOK OF ACTS

L uke was the medical doctor who traveled with Paul the apostle, and took care of Paul's medical needs. But he was more than a physician, Luke was a co-minister with Paul. He could preach, but only when Paul wasn't present. But Luke's most enduring ministry was writing—he wrote the Gospel of Luke, the Book of Acts, and the Book of Hebrews.

Today we catch Luke on an important mission for the welfare of Paul and the evangelistic team that traveled with the apostles.

Because Luke was over 60 years old, he puffed as he walked up the steep incline to the large villa on the top of the hill. A very strong but little church met in the villa. It was a small church because not many people lived in the high plains region. It was a strong, well-taught church, because the owner of the villa—Theophilus—was well read. He had many books in his personal library; several of them were copies of Scripture. He used these to teach his small flock.

Theophilus was the owner of the surrounding fields that could be seen in the distance. Theophilus had servants working in the fields to fill his barns with grain. Other servants delivered his produce in wagons to nearby towns, and some even delivered goods to ships in the harbor. Theophilus was a wealthy businessman with many business connections.

"I hope he is as generous this time as last time," Luke thought to himself.

Three years ago Luke had approached Theophilus for a gift—a large one—to support Paul who was then imprisoned in Caesarea, a fortress in the Holy Land. Paul and his team needed money to pay for essentials because they weren't receiving offerings while Paul was in prison. Paul wasn't preaching where gifts were given to him. Paul had been in jail for two years and it cost almost 10,000 pieces of silver to live.

"Of course I'll give some money to support Paul," was Theophilus' response last time Luke asked him for a gift. "But, I'm a wise business-man," Theophilus told Luke. Theophilus wanted to help Paul, but he also wanted something in return.

The last time Luke came to see Theophilus he said, "I'll give you all the money you need but I want you to write a book for me while Paul is in prison." Theophilus wanted Luke to travel the Holy Land to interview people who talked to Jesus or were healed by Jesus, and write it all down in a book.

During the last trip, Theophilus walked Luke into his large library. Every wealthy person had a room where they kept books. Some rich people just showed off their books as a matter of pride. Many others allowed their servants read their books when their daily tasks were over. But books were a passion for Theophilus, his parents loved to read so they named him Theophilus which means, "lover of wisdom."

"Ha," he laughed loudly, "I've read some of these books a dozen times."

Then Theophilus got serious, "After I became a follower of Jesus Christ, I invited Matthew the apostle to come visit my villa. I gathered all my servants in my great courtyard. The apostle Matthew preached and many of my servants began following Jesus Christ."

Theophilus told how the following evening he invited the owners and slaves from other estates to come to his courtyard to hear the message of Jesus Christ. Many became followers of Jesus Christ and the spacious courtyard became a church.

The villa was built in a large U shape, with a wall protecting the open end. The three spacious porches were perfect for protection from the hot sun or cold rain of winter. The protected courtyard gave the church privacy.

Theophilus told how each evening Matthew read from a manuscript he was writing on the life of Christ. "I had a servant who is my scribe copy Matthew's Gospel for me."

Then Theophilus told how blind Bartimaeus visited the church to tell of his healing; he had written an accurate account of his healing. The scribe copied the story to keep it in the library for the church.

Luke thought fondly of his first conversation with Theophilus because the rich land owner gave him copies of all his accounts of Jesus with the instruction, "Go write a complete record of the life of Jesus in perfect sequence so I can use it for preaching in my church."

Theophilus gave him 10,000 talents of silver to take care of Paul. Luke determined to write an account of Jesus' life and ministry that would be the most accurate and complete book available to the church. As Luke began writing, God added His Holy Spirit to Luke's efforts so that the book Luke wrote was described as Anothem which meant "from above."[1]

God's Holy Spirit had used Luke to write an inspired and inerrant Gospel that became part of the canon.

As Luke knocked on the front gate of the villa, he thought, "I wonder what Theophilus will want me to do this time?" Luke didn't ask for money right away. Like old friends, Luke and Theophilus reviewed their times together and Theophilus asked Luke to preach to his servants that evening. When most of the people in the villa had gone to sleep, Luke and Theophilus sat by a flickering candle in the library discussing things. Finally Theophilus asked, "Why have you come?"

Luke began to tell of the voyage of Paul from Caesarea to Rome. The Jews in Jerusalem had plotted to assassinate Paul, so the apostle had appealed to Caesar. Luke told all the details of the trip...Paul's sickness...the storm...the shipwreck...and Publius' father's healing and conversion. Then Luke turned his attention to Paul's condition.

"We must rent an apartment in Rome and feed the companions of Paul. Paul is chained to a guard and it will be two years before Caesar will hear his case."

"Ho, ho, ho," Theophilus laughed heartily. Not a skeptical laugh but a knowing laugh. Then he repeated himself from two years ago.

"You know I'm a careful businessman…" He paused long. Then looking into the physician's eyes said, "I want you to write a book, everything you just told me. My church needs to hear these stories of the church from the beginning. Begin the book with the Great Commission and Jesus' return to Heaven. Begin the book, "This is a continuation of all that Jesus began to do and teach. This book is the story of the Acts of the Apostles."

"I'll do that," Luke answered.

"Good…" Theophilus answered. "I'll use it in my preaching to my church. And who knows, maybe the Holy Spirit will inspire this one just like the first one.

Theophilus then winked at Luke, "Then I'll have my scribe make copies of it for the other churches."

Endnote

1. Luke 1:1-4.

Jesus Ascended Into Heaven

Acts 1:1-11

Lord, help me understand Your plan for my life
As I pray through the Book of Acts.
Fill me with the Holy Spirit so I can
Minister in resurrection power as did the early church.

Luke reminded Theophilus that his first letter
Told all what the human Jesus began to do and teach
While He was alive on earth.
This second letter would tell of the acts of the Holy Spirit
Through the disciples as they planted the early church.

After His death, Jesus returned to Heaven,
But during the 40 days after His crucifixion,
He appeared to the disciples from time to time
Where He prepared them for life-long ministry
And He demonstrated to them proofs of His deity.

In His last meeting with them in Jerusalem,
Jesus told them not to leave Jerusalem, but to
Pray until the Holy Spirit came upon them in power.
Jesus reminded them, "John the Baptist baptized with water,
In a few days I will baptize you with the Holy Spirit."
But the disciples didn't understand; they asked, "Lord,
Will You now restore the kingdom to free us from Rome?"
Jesus answered, "The Father has set that date, and
It's not for you to know."
Jesus said, "But take the Gospel into all the world when
The Holy Spirit is come upon you. Tell them about Me;
Beginning in Jerusalem, then Judaea, next Samaria, and finally
To the ends of the earth."
When Jesus finished, He was lifted into the sky

And disappeared into a cloud, leaving the disciples
Staring into the sky looking for Him.
Suddenly, two men in glistening white robes said to them,
"Why are you staring into the sky? Jesus has
Returned to Heaven, and one day He will return just as He left."

Lord, while Your glorified body is at the right hand
Of the throne of God in Heaven,
I know You are in my heart. Help me live
For You until You return.

Amen

The Story of the Ascension of Jesus to Heaven

The upper room was silent of everything except the voice of Jesus Christ. The eleven disciples sat motionlessly listening to Jesus. They couldn't take their eyes off Him. Jesus was the same human man they followed through the dusty roads of Galilee, yet He was the LORD God. He just appeared supernaturally among them when the doors were locked. Yet no one asked, "How did You get in?"

Jesus earlier had told them to go into all the world, not just to the land of Israel. Jesus had told them to preach to every one—not just the Jews. Jesus previously told them to baptize and teach all new converts.

Peter's red eyebrows reflected a questioning look. Then he blurted out, "What is our message? Should we tell people to 'follow You' just as we followed You?"

"You will preach to people the message of good news," Jesus explained. "Previously, people had to take a lamb to be sacrificed for forgiveness of their sins...I am the Lamb of God who takes away the sins of the world." The disciples remembered John the Baptist announcing Jesus was the Lamb of God.

At first the disciples did not understand the meaning of Jesus' death on the Cross. None expected Jesus to rise from the dead, so they didn't understand what the resurrection meant. Jesus explained, "Just as the lamb was the substitute for the sins of Israel, so I am the substitute for the sins of the world. Everyone should die under the judgment of God because of their sins, but I died in their place."

Jesus waited for His message to sink in, then He explained further, "When people accept Me as their Savior, I will forgive their sins."

Jesus stood to leave the upper room, the eleven also got to their feet. He told them, "As you go into all the world, preach the good news to everyone that I have died for their sins, and that I arose from the dead to give them new life—eternal life."

The piercing eyes of Jesus gazed from one disciple to another, "You have witnessed My death and resurrection, now tell everyone."

As they left the room Jesus added, "Announce to everyone they must repent from their sins and believe in Me to have their sins forgiven."

The disciples nodded that they understood.

Walking through the streets of Jerusalem, Jesus said to them, "Tarry here in Jerusalem and pray till the Holy Spirit comes on you."

The disciples understood Moses, Gideon, and Jeremiah—their heroes ministered with power when the Spirit of the Lord came upon them. They anticipated the same power.

"But you must pray to get power."

Jesus led them out of the city, walking toward the Mount of Olives. They walked passed the Temple and remembered when Jesus had cleansed it of moneychangers.

They shuttered when they walked passed Gethsemane, remembering this garden was the place where Jesus was arrested.

When they got to the top of the Mount of Olives, Peter asked the questions, "Will the kingdom be restored *now*?"

For 40 days Jesus had been teaching them about their ministry in all the world. Jesus had taught them what to preach. But the disciples were still confused. Their minds echoed Peter's question, "Lord, will You set up the kingdom now? Will You drive the Romans into the sea? Will the lion lay down with the lamb? Will righteousness roll down the hills as God's refreshing dew?"

Jesus stopped at the top of the mount to answer, "It is not for you to know when My Father will set up the kingdom—the 1,000 years of peace—it's for a future time."

Jesus explained, "I didn't come this time to sit on David's throne in Jerusalem," Jesus could still see disappointment in their eyes. They wanted to help drive the Romans out of the Holy Land. "I've come to sit on the throne of people's hearts." Jesus reminded them that was His message for the past three and a half years.

Jesus continued speaking, "Now here is your present focus, you will receive power when the Holy Spirit comes on you—after you pray 10 days—then you will be witnesses of My Gospel—first in Jerusalem, then in Judea, next in Samaria, and finally into all the world."

When Jesus finished speaking, He was lifted up into the sky. The disciples stood speechless. They saw Him going up as Elijah must have gone to Heaven. They were too speechless to yell...or ask if He was coming back...or what they should do now. They were transfixed at what they were seeing.

A cloud floated between them and Jesus. They no longer saw Him. Jesus was gone. "Why are you standing here?" two men in dazzling white robes asked them. They were angels who said, "He will return just as you have seen Him go."

The disciples remembered the last command of Jesus was to tarry in prayer in Jerusalem until the Holy Spirit came on them. They headed toward the city and to the upper room. They would wait and pray.

Praying in the Upper Room

Acts 1:12-26

Lord, it must have been perplexing to other disciples when Jesus left them.
Be with me, let me always feel Your presence.

The disciples walked a half mile back into Jerusalem
     And began praying in the upper room as Jesus instructed.
The disciples present were Peter, John, James, Andrew,
     Philip, Thomas, Bartholomew, Matthew, James, the son of
     Alphaeus, Simon the Zealot and Judas, son of James.
Several women were there, including Mary the mother of Jesus;
     There were 120 present and
     They prayed for 10 days.

Finally, Peter stood to address the group, "Brothers, it is necessary
     For us to fulfill the scriptures about Judas
     Who betrayed Jesus by guiding the mob to arrest Him."
It was predicted what we should do by the Holy Spirit through David,
     "He (Judas) was chosen just as we were, and had part
     In our ministry, but he lifted up his heel against us."
Judas purchased a field with the money he stole from us
     And he plunged to his death in that field;
     All his bowels spilled on the ground.
The news of his death circulated among the people, and
     They called it the Field of Blood.
King David also predicted in Psalms, "Let his home
     Be desolate, and let no one live there, and
     Let his work be given to someone else."
Peter said they should choose someone to take Judas' place
     And join them as witnesses of Jesus' resurrection.
"Let us choose someone who has been with us since
     The baptism of John and must have seen
     The physically resurrected Jesus

And been with us since the ascension."
They nominated two men: Joseph Justus (also called Barsabbas) and
Matthias;
> Then they prayed that the right man would be chosen, saying,
"O Lord, You know their hearts, show us which of these
> Men you have chosen as an apostle to replace
> Judas, the traitor, who has gone to his place."
Then they cast lots and Matthias' lot was chosen,
> And he was numbered with the eleven.

Lord, I want to follow You; keep me close to Your side.
> *May I never betray You as did Judas, nor may I*
> *Embarrass You as did Peter by denying You.*

Amen

The Coming of the Holy Spirit

Acts 2:1-13

Lord, when I read of the Holy Spirit empowering the disciples,
> *I want the same Holy Spirit in my life;*
> *I want His power in my service for You.*

When the day of Pentecost had come—seven weeks and one day
> Since the Passover when Jesus died—
> They were still praying in unity in the upper room.
Suddenly they heard a great noise that sounded like a wind storm
> That filled the room where they were praying;
> But they were not blown about, nor was the room disrupted.
They saw flames of fire in the air, and it settled
> On each of them, but no one was burned.
And they were all filled with the Holy Spirit and
> All began to speak in foreign languages they didn't know;
> The Holy Spirit gave them this miraculous ability.

Many obedient Jews were in Jerusalem for Pentecost,
    Having come from many nations of the earth.
When they heard the noise of the mighty wind,
    They came to see what was going on.
They were surprised to hear their own tongue
    Being spoken by the disciples.
"How can this be," they asked, "these men are from Galilee,
    Yet we hear them speaking fluently in our language?"
They were Parthians, and Medes, and Elamites, and those who
    Live in Mesopotamia and Judea, and Cappadocia,
In Pontus and Asia, Phrygia and Pamphylia,
    In Egypt, and in parts of Libya near Cyrene,
    And visitors from Rome, both Jews and Jewish converts, Cretans
    and Arabians.
They exclaimed, "We hear them tell the wonderful works of God
    In our mother tongue."
They were amazed and asked one another, "What does this mean?"
    Others in the crowd mocked the disciples, saying,
    "They are drunk with new wine."

Lord, help me tell everyone what You've
    Done for me, just as the disciples did.
May I never keep silent because I'm afraid
    What the crowd will think or say.

Amen

Peter Preaching at Pentecost

Acts 2:14-39

Peter with the eleven disciples stood before the crowd to answer them,
    "Listen you people of Judah, and all who live in Jerusalem,
These are not drunk as you suppose,

It is too early, it's only 9 o'clock in the morning."
"What you see is what was predicted by Joel the prophet,
    'In the last days,' God said,
'I will pour out my Spirit on all mankind
    And your sons and daughters shall prophesy,
    And your young men shall see visions,
    And your old men shall dream dreams.'
    'And I will cause miracles in Heaven and earth,
    The sun shall become black, and the moon blood red
    Before the awesome Day of the Lord arrives.'
    'And all who call on the name of the Lord
    Shall be saved.'"

"Listen, men of Israel! You know God publicly endorsed
    Jesus of Nazareth by doing miracles through Him."
    "God pre-determined for you to deliver Jesus
    To the Roman government to murder Him
    By nailing Him to a cross,
    Then God released Him from the grip of death
    And brought Him back to life again
    Because death could not keep Jesus in the grave."

"David predicted this resurrection when he said,
    'I saw the LORD before me, He is always
    By my side, so that I shall not be shaken.'
'Therefore, my heart is filled with rejoicing and
    My tongue shouts praise to God because I
    Know God will take care of me in death.'
    'You will not leave my soul in Hell, neither will
    You let Your Holy Son decay in the grave.'
    'You will give me back my physical life
    And fill me with joy as I stand in Your presence.'"

Peter continued preaching saying David was dead
    And buried and his tomb was in Jerusalem, yet

David was a prophet who said,
"God has sworn in an oath that Messiah would be
His descendent and sit on the throne." Seeing the future,
David said, "Messiah would not be abandoned to the grave,
Even His body would not suffer decay. We are witnesses,
That God has raised Jesus to new life,
Then He was exalted to the right hand of God and
Received by the Father."
"Then God poured out the promised Holy Spirit as
Evidenced by what you see and hear among His followers."

Then Peter referred to David again "For David did not ascend
To Heaven, yet he quoted the Messiah Who said,
'The Lord said to my Lord,
Sit at My right hand until I make Your enemies Your footstool.
"Therefore, all Israel should realize God the Father
Has made Jesus—whom you crucified—both Lord and Messiah."

The people were cut to the heart when they heard this
And asked, "What shall we do?"
Peter answered, "Repent, so your sins will be forgiven and be baptized
Every one of you in the name of the Lord, Jesus Christ,
And you will receive the gift of the Holy Spirit;
This promise is for you, your children, and those in distant lands
Who will call upon the Lord our God."

Lord, Peter preached a powerful sermon at Pentecost;
Help me witness for You according to my ability,
And according to my opportunity.

Amen

The New Church Was Born

Acts 2:40-47

Peter preached a long sermon featuring Jesus, urging
>All of his listeners to, "Save yourself from the
>Punishment that's coming upon this nation."

And approximately 3,000 were baptized and joined them;
>They regularly attended the apostle's teachings, and
>The Lord's Table, and prayer meetings.

A deep awe came on them as many miracles
>Were done by the apostles.

The believers had everything in common,
>Selling their possessions to give to anyone who had need.

They met together everyday in the Temple courtyards
>And broke bread together in homes and shared meals
>With great joy and thankfulness, praising God.

The unsaved were favorable to the believers, and daily God added
>To the church as people were being saved.

Lord, thank You for the outpouring of the Holy Spirit that draws
>*Unsaved people to Jesus Christ. Thank You for saving me.*
>*Continue pouring Your Holy Spirit on me so others can be saved.*

Amen

Healing a Man Born Crippled

Acts 3:1-11

Lord, give me a passion to pray at all times,
>*With all people, at all places, for all requests,*
>*In all the various ways You've taught us to pray.*

Peter and John went into the Temple at 3:00 P.M. to

>Pray with all those seeking to call on Your name.

They encountered a lame man at the gate who had

>Never walked in his life, friends brought him there daily.

He was begging for alms from worshipers so he asked

>Peter and John for a gift of charity.

Peter looked directly at him and said, "Look at us!"

>So the lame man looked at them,

>Expecting to receive some money.

Then Peter said, "I don't have any silver or gold,

>But I'll give you what I have. In the name of

>Jesus Christ of Nazareth, rise up and walk."

Then Peter grabbed him by the hand and pulled him

>To his feet. Immediately his feet and ankles were strengthened.

He leaped up and walked into the Temple with them;

>He was leaping and dancing and shouting praises to God.

The worshipers saw him walking and leaping and

>Recognized he was the lame man who begged at the gate,

>So the crowd was surprised and curious.

The other worshipers rushed into Solomon's porch to see the healed man;

>They stood in awe at the miracle that just happened.

Lord, I stand in awe of Your miracle-working power;

>*Thank You for healing the crippled man at the Temple gate.*

Help me believe You today for other healing events

>*And give me the prayer of faith to pray for those who are sick.*

Amen

Peter's Sermon in Response

Acts 3:12-26

Peter realized it was an opportunity to preach, so he said,
     "Men of Israel, why are you surprised and why are you
     Staring at us as though we did this?"
     "The God of our fathers has done this miracle, the God of Abraham,
     Isaac and Jacob has done this to honor His servant, Jesus."
     "You betrayed Jesus and denied Him before Pilate,
     Even when Pilate decided to let Him go."
Peter preached straight at them, "You disowned the righteous Jesus
     And begged for Pilate to give you a murderer instead."
     "You were responsible for the death of Christ, but God
     Raised Him from the dead. John and I
     Are witnesses of this truth, we saw Him alive."
     "This man was healed in the name of Jesus.
     It was faith in Christ Jesus that gave this man
     His health and healing, and all of you can see it."
     "I realize that you had no idea what
     The Jewish leaders were doing to Jesus Christ,
     But the prophets foretold that Messiah would suffer,
     And through your blindness this came about."
     "Now you must repent and turn to God so that your sins
     Can be forgiven, and so God can send to you
     Times of refreshing that come from the presence of God."
     "Then God will send Jesus Your Messiah back to you;
     But for now, He must remain in Heaven
     Until the final restoration of all things."
     "This is the prediction of Moses who said, 'The Lord God
     Will raise up a prophet like me; listen to all His messages.'
     'Every soul that will not listen to that prophet
     Shall be utterly destroyed.'"
Peter continued preaching, "All the prophets from Samuel

Onward have predicted these days."

"You are the sons of the prophets who have predicted these

Things, and heirs of the covenant that God made with

Abraham that

'Through you shall all the families of the earth be blessed.'"

"It was you who God first wanted to bless through His Son Jesus

After He had raised Him from the dead

By forgiving the sins of every one of you."

But many believed who heard what they said,

So that about 5,000 men now believed.

Lord, I'm encouraged when lives are changed with the Gospel

And the outward number of believers grows.

Amen

The Apostles Arrested

Acts 4:1-3

While Peter and John were talking to the people, the chief priest,

Captain of the Temple Guard, and some Sadducees

Were disturbed that they preached Jesus had risen from the dead,

So they arrested them and put them in jail for the night.

Lord, I know You came first for the salvation of the Jews,

But I'm glad You provide salvation for all Gentiles...

But most of all for me.

Amen

Peter and John Before the Jewish Leaders

Acts 4:5-12

The next day, the council of Jewish leaders convened in Jerusalem
  With Annas the High Priest, Caiaphas, John, Alexander
  And others of the high priest's relatives.
Then the two disciples were brought in before them
  And were asked, "By what name or authority have you done this?"
Peter, filled with the Holy Spirit, answered, "Leaders and Elders,
  Are you questioning us about the kindness
  Done to a crippled man, and how he was healed?"
  "It is high time that you leaders and all Israel realize this miracle
  Was done in the name of Jesus Christ of Nazareth!"
  "He is the One you crucified, but God raised Him from the dead;
  And by the power of Jesus this man stands here healed."
  "Jesus is the Stone which you builders rejected, but now
  He has become the Cornerstone of the building."
  "Neither is there salvation in any other;
  There is no other name
  Under Heaven given among people, whereby we must be saved."

Lord, give me boldness like Peter to witness for Jesus,
  Especially to those who don't believe in Him.

Amen

The Jewish Leaders Forbid Preaching in Jesus' Name

Acts 4:13-22

The Jewish leaders were amazed at the boldness of Peter and John
  Because they were uneducated and ignorant men;
  The leaders realized they had been with Jesus
But they could not say anything against the disciples

Because the healed man was standing with them.
So the leaders ordered the disciples to leave the council
    So they could discuss the issue among themselves saying,
"What are we going to do with these men?"
        "It is evident to everyone in Jerusalem that an outstanding
        Miracle has been done by these men, and we can't deny it."
"Nevertheless, to prevent this thing from spreading, let's
        Command them not to speak in His name again."
So they called Peter and John and commanded them not to
        Speak anymore in the name of Jesus.
Peter and John answered them, "We have to decide whether
        God wants us to listen to you, more than to Him;
        We cannot stop telling everyone what we have seen and heard."
After more threats, they let Peter and John go
        Because they didn't know how to punish them any further.
The people supported them wholeheartedly, glorifying God
        For the miracle on the man who was over 40 years old.

Lord, all life is in Your hands, I praise You for good health;
        I praise You for times when You heal and times when You don't.

Amen

The Church Prays

Acts 4:23-31

When the apostles were released, they went back to the believers
        And reported what the chief priest and elders said to them;
        The Christians raised their voices to God in praise,
"Almighty Lord, You have made Heaven and earth, the seas and
        Everything in them; You spoke by the Holy Spirit through David,

        'Why do the heathen rage,
        And the people imagine sinful things,

The kings of the earth unite to fight You,
And oppose the Messiah, Your Son?'"

"For in this city of Jerusalem, the rulers have united to fight
Against your holy servant, Jesus, the Anointed One."
"Herod, and Pontius Pilate, and the Roman soldiers, and the people of Israel,
Have gathered together to carry out what You
Had previously planned to happen."
"Now Lord, listen to their threats and give to us, Your servants,
Boldness to speak Your Word courageously."
"Continue to stretch out Your hand to heal and do miracles
In the name of Your Holy Servant, Jesus."
When they had finished praying, the room was shaken
And they were all filled with the Holy Spirit
And they spoke the Word of God boldly.

Lord, I want to speak boldly for You;
Fill me with the Holy Spirit and courage.

Amen

The Story of Barnabas: The Rich Young Ruler

A man with a smile as big as his frame walked among the Christians as they waited for a prayer meeting to start. He was tall, huge-shouldered, and heavy, but not fat. He was always well dressed in the finest of clothing and his beard was immaculately manicured.

No one in the church knew when Barnabas was converted. He didn't follow Jesus before the cross and he wasn't one of those who was converted and baptized on the day of Pentecost. Then one day his story came out.

This man was the rich young ruler who had gone to Jesus to ask, "Good, Master, what shall I do to inherit eternal life?"

At first, Jesus corrected him saying, "Why are you calling Me good? There is none good but God." But the rich young ruler would not back off, he kept asking, "What must I do to go to Heaven?"

Jesus answered, "You know the commandments, obey them and you shall live. Do not commit adultery, do not kill, do no steal, do not lie, and honor your father and mother."

But there was something in this big man's eyes. The rich young ruler knew that he had kept all the commandments outwardly, but his heart betrayed him; he knew he was not right with God. He answered, "I have done all these things since I was a child, but I am not sure I am going to Heaven."

Jesus looked on him and loved him; then answered, "You only lack one thing, sell all that you have, give to the poor, and come and follow Me."

When the young ruler heard this he nodded only because he understood what Jesus meant. But the more he thought about his money, and his real estate holdings, and all of his clothing, he knew that is was impossible to give them up. Then he began slowly shaking his head "no."

"I can't do it," his eyes were sad. He turned and began walking away.

Jesus commented to the crowd, "It's hard for rich people to enter the kingdom of Heaven, it's easier for a camel to go through the eye of a needle than for a rich man to enter into Heaven."

The big man was a Levite, this was the Jewish tribe set aside to serve God in the Temple. Some Levites were priests who offered animal sacrifices, other Levites were teachers, and still others took care of the physical things of the Temple. God had commanded that the Levites could not own property or acquire wealth; they were to live off the tithes and offerings that worshipers brought to the Temple.[1] And when people brought their animals to sacrifice, parts of the animals were given to the Levites to feed their families. God didn't want the greed of riches to choke the ministry of those who serve Him in the Temple.

The rich young ruler owned property. He knew that money deprived him of fellowship with God. His love of money deprived him of entrance into the kingdom of Heaven.

Sometime after meeting Jesus and after the birth of the church, the rich young ruler—named Barnabas—made a decision to sell everything and follow Jesus. It wasn't a dramatic decision, nor did he make it in front of the new growing community called the church. It was a decision made deep in the recesses of his heart.

When the church people gathered to listen to the Word of God, Barnabas came into the assembly with a large sack. No one paid much attention to the sack.

"Is there anything anyone else wants to say?" the red-headed Peter asked the young congregation before dismissing them. It was then when Barnabas made his way to the front of the meeting, and then kneeling before the apostles, laid a large sack of money on the floor at their feet.

"What is this?" Peter, speaking for the crowd, wondering, "What's in the bag?"

"The fruit of my repentance," was all Barnabas could say. Then he confessed that he was a Levite who had illegally owned property on the Island of Cyprus. "I sold it, and I want to give the money to Jesus Christ."

Without asking the other apostles or the congregation, Peter spoke for them all, "The money will go to take care of the widows who are among us." Everyone shook their head in agreement.

Peter walked over to a table with the heavy sack and poured the money out and the clatter could be heard by all as the coins fell on the top of the table.

"OOh-OOh-OOh," the people marveled at the amount of money. It was a lot more than most of the poor people had ever seen in one place. Then they broke into a cheer and applauded loudly. It was both an appreciation to Barnabas for giving the money as well as an applause to God who had provided resources for the young church.

Ananias was sitting on the first row—seats reserved for spiritual leaders—and when he saw all the money, he immediately thought of what he could do with that money, if it were his. Then he thought of buying large quantities of olive oil from the outlying districts and bringing it to Jerusalem for quite a profit.

Later that night, Ananias and Sapphira talked about the public response to the gift of Barnabas. After the meeting was over, the men patted Barnabas on the back, congratulating him. Then they gave Barnabas a seat of honor among the elders; they advanced Barnabas ahead of Ananias. It was a seat Ananias wanted. Sapphira commented, "If you have the seat where Barnabas is now sitting, all the other women would look up to me..." Ananias and Sapphira wanted to give to the church but in return, they wanted Christians to "pat" them on the back as they had done Barnabas. Then they hatched a plan.

"I am going to sell all my fields up in Ramar," Ananias said to his wife, "then I'll place the money at the elders' feet just as Barnabas did. My sack of money will be just as big as his sack of money and the church will rejoice in that gift, and they'll appreciate us."

Then Ananias thought of those flasks of olive oil and how he could make money selling them in Jerusalem. Then he suggested an idea to his wife, "I'll keep back a little money to buy some olive oil up in Ramar, and bring it down to Jerusalem to sell it and make a profit." Sapphira nodded her head in approval. Then Ananias added, "For a short period of time we could make enough money to replenish what we gave away and then sometime in the future, we can give that amount of money a second time." Again, Sapphira nodded her head.

Endnote

1. Deuteronomy 18:1-2.

The Church Prospers

Acts 4:32-37

All of the believers were one heart and mind and
    No one was selfish with their possessions, but
    Shared freely, as though their things belonged to all.
The apostles continued witnessing boldly the resurrection of the Lord Jesus,

And there was a wonderful spirit of fellowship among them all,
    And there was not a single believer in need of anything.
Those who owned property, sold it and brought the proceeds
    And placed them at the apostles' feet; then
    Distribution was made to all in need.
Joseph was given the name Barnabas by the apostles
        (a name meaning exhorter);
    Barnabas was a Levite who broke the Mosaic Law by owning land,
    So he sold his farm in Cyprus and gave it to the church.

Lord, teach me to be unselfish with all I own. I give it to You.
    Guide me how I should spend all my money
    Because everything belongs to You.

Amen

The Sin and Judgment of Ananias and Sapphira

Acts 5:1-11

Another man who owned property named Ananias
    Agreed with his wife Sapphira to sell it
    But they kept back part of the price for themselves.
Ananias placed the remaining money at the apostles' feet,
    But Peter said, "Why have you let satan fill
    Your heart to cheat the Holy Spirit?"
"Why have you kept part of the price for the land?"
    "...The land didn't need to be sold, it was yours;
    The price for the land was also yours."
"Why have you thought you could deceive God?
    You have not lied to the church, you've lied to God!"
When Ananias heard this condemnation, he collapsed and died;
    All who heard it were terrified. The young men
    Covered him with a sheet, and then buried him.

About three hours later, his wife came into the assembly
 Not knowing what happened to her husband.
Peter asked her, "Did you sell your land for so much?"
 "Yes," she answered, "that was the price."
Peter asked, "Why did you agree to cheat the Holy Spirit?"
 The young men who buried your husband are at the door";
 Immediately, she collapsed and died.
The young men buried her next to her husband;
 Terror gripped the young church and no one
 Was tempted to lie or cheat God in any way.

Lord, give me a godly fear of telling a lie or
 Doing anything to cheat the Holy Spirit. Keep me honest.

Amen

Victory in the Early Church

Acts 5:12-16

The apostles were meeting regularly at Solomon's porch
 In the Temple, doing miracles among the people.
But some were afraid to join them for the wrong reasons.
 The believers were well respected by people in general.
As a result more and more became believers
 In growing numbers, men and women.
Many signs and wonders were being done by the apostles;
 As a result, people brought the sick to the streets
 And laid them down so Peter's shadow might fall on them.
A large crowd of people came from other cities,
 Bringing their sick and those who were demon possessed,
 So they could be healed by the apostles.

Lord, keep me excited with the work of evangelism
 So that many people become Christians by my ministry.

Amen

The Second Persecution

Acts 5:17-42

The high priest and the Sadducees reacted to the
>Work of the apostles, and in jealousy, had the apostles
>Arrested and put in a common prison.

But an angel of the Lord came at night and opened the door
>And led them out, telling them; "Go stand in the
>Temple and tell people about the Christian life."

About sun up they went into the Temple and began to preach;
>Later the members of the Sanhedrin arrived, and gathered the
>Senate and sent for the apostles to come from the jail.

The officers could not find them in the prison. They reported,
>"We founded the jail locked, and guards on duty, but when
>We opened the door, no one was there."

The Sanhedrin was mystified, wondering what happened to
>Their prisoners. Then someone arrived to announce that the
>Prisoners were preaching in the Temple.

The captain went with guards to get them, but didn't
>Use any violence because they feared the crowd,
>So they brought them to the Sanhedrin.

The high priest said, "We gave you strict orders not to teach
>In this name, but you have filled Jerusalem with your
>Teaching, and accused us of the death of Jesus."

Peter replied, "We must obey God and not men. The
>God of our fathers raised up Jesus from the dead because
>You had Him executed on a wooden Roman cross."

"God has exalted this man to His own right hand
>As Prince and Savior, for the forgiveness of Israel's sin."

"We are witnesses of the resurrection and so is the Holy Spirit
>Whom God has given to those who obey Him."

When the Sanhedrin heard this, they were furious and wanted to
        execute them
      But Gamaliel, a Pharisee and teacher greatly respected by all,
      Stood and gave orders for the apostles to be taken outside.
Gamaliel said, "Men and brethren, be careful what action you take
      Against these men. Remember, a man named Theudus who
      Claimed to be something great? He had a following of 400 men."
"When Theudus was killed, his followers were dispersed and the threat
        was gone;
      Also remember Judas who had a great following. When Judas
        was killed,
      His followers dispersed."
"I suggest you leave the apostles alone;
      If their movement is of men, it will break up of its own accord."
"If their movement is of God, you can't do anything about it,
      And you may find yourself fighting against God";
      The advice of Gamaliel was accepted.
They called in the apostles and warned them not to preach in this name;
      Then they flogged them and let them go.
The apostles left the Sanhedrin rejoicing, because
      They had been counted worthy to suffer for the name of Jesus.
Day after day, they did not cease preaching and teaching Jesus Christ
      From house to house and in the Temple courts.

Lord, thank You for the courage and boldness of the early church.
      May I always live for You with the same level of courage.
Thank You for using the early church to reach people for Jesus;
      Use me as a witness in the lives of lost people.

Amen

The Story of Choosing Seven Deacons

The young church was growing rapidly. Every day people were being converted to Jesus Christ and added to the young church. The apostles were going house to house praying with family groups and celebrating the Lord's Table. Every time a new family came to know Christ, it expanded the work of the apostles.

As more families became Christians, more widows were added to the church roll. The compassionate church wanted to do something for the widows. People were selling everything they had and donating it to the church. The young church had all things in common. So, the young church began feeding their widows every day. Families would cook extra food for them, along with their meals. Clothing was bought for the widows as well as provision for their needs.

Around noon each day in Hezekiah's court, many of the apostles came together to dispense to the widows the food that was brought for them. Several tables were set up and different kinds of food were placed on each table. Some had large pots of food, others had sacks of bread and other tables held clothing for the widows.

"Line up!" Peter yelled to all the ladies who were crowding up to the tables. Then he yelled louder, "LINE UP." Peter had to yell over the crowd. He wanted to restore order before distributing the food. He began praying, "Let's pray." And every head quickly was bowed in silent reverence. Peter prayed, *"Blessed are You, Lord, our God, King of the Universe...."* These are the beginning words of prayer a Jewish male would have used to thank God for the food.

As quickly as Peter said "AMEN," the ladies erupted into a hub-bub of conversation, and they began pushing to the head of the line. They knew that certain pots of food were better than others. Most knew that Sarah used more roasted lamb in her stew than others. So every woman elbowed her way toward Sarah's stew.

Other women elbowed their way toward certain breads that were baked with a hard crust and still warm from the oven. No one wanted bread that was sometimes two or three days old, and a little stale. Even before lining up, women began to "eye" the food on the tables. Some women tried to touch the breads to find out which ones were still warm.

"KEEP BACK, STAY IN LINE…" Peter again yelled to the women. Some of the other disciples had to stand in a row to keep the women in line.

It took almost an hour of the apostles' time to gather the food, guard the table, and guide the widows through the line. It was so frustrating that Peter asked, "Who wants to try to control crabby women?" Young John wanted to spend more time in prayer noting, "It's not right that we have to come away from our prayers and preaching the Word of God to serve the widows their daily food."

"Yes!" the other disciples nodded in agreement.

Then one of the widows complicated the problem. She yelled out—this complaining Jewish widow who was born outside the Holy Land, "We have to stand in the back of the line because the "holy" widows from the Holy Land get first place in line." The other Hellenistic widows—those from outside the Holy Land—murmured in agreement. It was easy to identify the Hellenistic widows by their dialect and the clothing they wore.

The Hellenistic widows glared at the "holy" widows from the Holy Land, and they glared back. A few mean words were spoken under their breath and both sides could be seen turning their shoulders away from the others in disgust.

"The 'holy' women from the Holy Land are not so 'holy,'" was heard from the criticizing Hellenistic widows.

In that moment, Peter realized there was a problem in the early church. The harmony in the young Body of Christ was broken. Peter could hear it in the tone of their voices, and could see it in some "mean-spirited" eyes. Peter didn't like what he saw. He knew he had to do something because this new "Body of Christ" had been characterized by harmony and unity. Peter remembered how they prayed together earnestly in the upper room for the Holy Spirit to come upon them. Originally, they had only one voice before God, now they were divided with criticism.

Turning to the others, Peter asked, "What are we going to do about this problem?" Peter motioned for them to come with him to pray for an answer from the Holy Spirit. They had to do something before this festering sore contaminated the whole body.

The disciples found a room to pray and fell on their faces, confessing the sins of early greed and selfishness. Philip voiced their concern, "Oh, Lord, what can we do...how can we repent...how can we become unified before an unbelieving world?"

"That's it," Peter announced to the other men who still had their heads bowed in prayer. Peter said that Philip's prayer was the answer to their problem. "We must repent of our sin," Peter announced to the other disciples.

"We must repent by not only telling God we're sorry, but by telling the Hellenistic widows we're sorry." Peter suggested that they appoint seven Hellenistic servants to daily supervise giving food to the widows. Peter explained that these Hellenistic servants should not be from the Holy Land, but rather, these seven servants must be Hellenistic Jews since it was the Hellenistic widows who were complaining.

"If we bend over backward to satisfy this criticism," Peter noted, "then we'll make sure that everyone gets an equal share every day."

Internal Problems in the Early Church

Acts 6:1-7

Even though believers were multiplying in the early church,
> There were rumblings of discontent among them.
The Hellenistic widows born outside the Holy Land
> Were complaining about the Jewish widows born in the Holy Land,
Because they were being discriminated against,
> When food was daily passed out to those in need.
The twelve apostles called the multitude of Christians together
> And explained that it was not appropriate for them

To spend their time supervising a humanitarian hot food
kitchen.
They explained, "Look around and pick seven men
Of good reputation, practical minded, and filled with
The Holy Spirit and faith who can administer this program."
"We will spend our time in prayer
And preaching the Word of God."
There was unanimous approval from the multitude
So they bent over backward and chose seven Hellenistic men
Beginning with Stephen because he was filled with the Holy Spirit.
They also chose Philip, Prochorus, Nicanor, Timon,
Parmenas, and Nicholas of Antioch who had
Just become a Christian.
These seven men were brought before the apostles
Who laid their hands upon them and committed them to God.
As a result, the Word of God reached a larger circle of listeners
And the number of disciples multiplied greatly.
Also, a number of priests—those who hated Christianity—were saved
When they saw how the early church handled
Its money problems and internal griping.

Lord, thank You that the early church repented
And bent over backward to deal with criticism.
May I always go-the-extra-mile when criticized
To show others the spirit of forgiveness and compassion.

Amen

The Ministry of Stephen the Deacon

Acts 6:8-15

Stephen, a deacon filled with the Holy Spirit and power,
Worked miracles and signs among the masses.

He got opposition from the synagogues of freemen,
Hellenistic Jews from Cyrene, Alexandria, Cilicia and Asia.
They debated with Stephen, but couldn't answer his
Wisdom and spirit. So the freemen brought in
Men to lie, saying Stephen cursed Moses and God.
This stirred up the people and elders and teachers of the law
So they seized Stephen and brought him
Before the Sanhedrin to face false witnesses,
Who said Stephen spoke against the Holy Spirit and the law,
Also claiming Stephen said, "Jesus will destroy the Temple
And change the customs handed down by Moses."
The members of the Sanhedrin saw Stephen's face
Become as radiant as an angel's face.

Lord, when I take a bold stand against Your enemies,
May they experience Your love flowing through my life
And may they see Your beauty in my countenance.

Amen

The Story of Stephen

The scene was chaotic. Curious spectators came running to see him die, young zealous Levites quickly picked up rocks to join the fracas; the crowd was screaming for blood. The women were chanting,

"STONE HIM...STONE HIM...STONE HIM..."

Stephen, a leader in the new sect of the way, was a follower of Jesus. Blood trickled from his mouth. His arms were raised to ward off the rocks. An open gash on the back of his head was throbbing.

The crowd was not punishing him because he was a follower of Jesus Christ, they hated him because he had debated the Jewish teachers of the law and won. Stephen was a Jew from outside the Holy Land where he was learned in Gentile logic. The Sanhedrin had not previously faced the arguments of Stephen who interpreted the Old Testament from a Gentile point of view. So the defeated Levites beat him with their fists as they were dragging him out of the Temple.

"DRAG HIM TO THE VALLEY OF HINNON AND STONE HIM!"

"YES...," was the mob's reply.

At first they were just going to punish him, but the smell of blood in the nose of a predator spurs it to the kill. By the time they yelled to stone him, murder was the assumed conclusion in the minds of everyone.

Saul, a young member of the Sanhedrin, was not at the debate. He, like Stephen, was born outside the Holy Land. He could have answered the logic of Stephen. Saul was a Jew from Tarsus in Asia, a city of liberal education and a center of the arts. Saul was brilliant in debate because he brought a fresh interpretation to the Law. When Saul heard the clamor of the crowd; he came running.

"HERE..." Saul yelled to the stone-throwers, "I'll hold your tunics."

Saul watched the punishing stones, some missing. But no one defended the martyr, no one quieted the crowd, no one came to his rescue. The leader of the Sanhedrin arrived; the action stopped momentarily when the elderly entourage got there. Everyone looked to the leader for permission to continue, the old Jewish leader had been hastily summoned; he did not have on his official garments. He asked those assembled, "Has this man done something worthy of death?"

It was a question that would not be answered, at least not out loud. Saul thought, "Kill these Christians because they blaspheme God...because they won't bring a sacrificial lamb...because they say Jesus is God...because they do miracles by magic...because they claim Jesus arose from the dead."

Saul wanted Stephen to die, just as Jesus was killed; but no cross to make Stephen a hero, as the Christians made Jesus a legend.

The crowd stood sober...waiting...ready. Then the leader of the Sanhedrin asked again,

"Has this man done anything worthy of death?"

"YES!" the old members of the Sanhedrin yelled first.

"YES!" the other members joined in the vote.

"YES!" shouted young Saul who was glad to see a Christian die.

One stone was thrown, Stephen put up a hand to divert it away. Then three or four stones were thrown at the same time, he couldn't divert them all. A rock thrown from the rear hit Stephen in the head.

THUD.

Stephen knew it was over. Already on his knees, he looked to Heaven to pray,

"Lord Jesus…" peace came over his face, "Lord, forgive their sin…I pray for them…save them."

Even those who hated him most, momentarily stopped their assault to hear what he was saying. Stephen looked into the sky…he saw Jesus, but the crowd thought he was just looking up. Saul didn't see anything but he was just interested in the last words of this man before he died. Most historians analyze the last words before death, for they usually reveal what a man truly believes, and how he lived.

Stephen looked into Heaven. He saw Jesus sitting at the right hand of the throne of God, and Stephen recognized Jesus. Although he had not seen the Master with his physical eyes, he recognized Him in death because he had prayed to Him so many times. Jesus began walking toward Stephen as a person goes to meet a friend, Stephen reached out to Jesus. Saul heard his prayer, so did everyone in the rock quarry, although no one saw Jesus but Stephen. Saul looked up to see what Stephen was staring at, he saw nothing. Stephen cried out,

"Lord Jesus…receive my spirit."

Stephen died a martyr's death, but rocks did not smash the breath from his lungs. The Lord Jesus took him.

The Sermon by Stephen

Acts 7:1-52

The high priest asked if the charges against Stephen were true;
  Stephen answered, "My brother and father listen to me,
The God of glory appeared to Abraham while he was in Mesopotamia.
  Before Abraham went to Haran, God said,
'Leave your country and family and go to a land I will show you;'
  So Abraham left Chaldea and settled in Haran,
  Staying there until his father died."
"Then Abraham left to come to this land where we now live today
  But God did not give him the land while he was alive,
But promised to give it to him and his descendents,
  Even though he was childless when the promise was made."
"Then God told him, 'Your descendents will be strangers
  In a foreign country, where they will become slaves
  And be oppressed for 400 years.'"
"God promised to judge the nation that enslaved them, then
  God promised His people would worship Him in this land."

Lord, Stephen thought it was important to show
  That You spoke to people who were not in the Promised Land.
Since You spoke to people before they entered the Promised Land,
  That meant now You could offer salvation to Gentiles outside
  The Promised Land.
Stephen was laying a foundation to prove You would bless
  The apostles as they went to preach to every person,
  Beginning at Jerusalem, then going to Judea, Samaria, and the world.

Stephen continued preaching,
  "God made a covenant of circumcision with them, so Isaac
  Was circumcised on the eighth day."
  "Isaac did the same for Jacob, and Jacob did it
  For his twelve sons who became the twelve patriarchs."

"The patriarchs were jealous of Joseph and sold him
Into slavery in Egypt, but God was with him."
"God rescued Joseph and made him wise enough to get
Pharaoh's attention who then made him governor of Egypt."

Lord, You called Your servant Joseph to serve You but
The Jewish establishment rejected Him,
Just as they rejected Jesus.
Lord, this helps me understand why
The religious establishment
Rejects Jesus today.

Stephen continued preaching,
"When famine caused suffering and devastation throughout
Egypt and Canaan, our ancestors had nothing to eat."
"When Jacob heard there was grain for sale in Egypt, he sent his
Ten sons there on their first visit to buy food."
"On the second visit, Joseph made himself known
To his brothers, and then told Pharaoh about his family."
"Jacob went to live in Egypt, where he and his family died;
Their bones were brought back and buried at Shechem
In the tomb Abraham purchased from Hamor, the father of
Shechem."

Lord, when I read how enemies persecuted Your people in Scripture,
It helps me understand why the world
Persecutes Your people today.

Stephen continued preaching,
"The nation of Israel grew larger in Egypt. A new king
Took the throne who didn't know Joseph. He oppressed
Our people and victimized our ancestors,
Forcing parents to abandon their babies."
"During this time Moses was born, he was no ordinary child;
For three months he was cared for at home."

"But when Moses was exposed to Pharaoh's daughter
She adopted him and raised him as her own child."
"Moses was taught all the wisdom of the Egyptians
And became mighty in speech and actions."
"At the age of forty he decided to visit his Jewish people;
He saw one of his fellow countrymen being abused
And defended him by killing the Egyptian."
"Moses thought the Jews would understand that
God would use him to deliver them;
But they didn't understand, nor respond positively to him."
"The next day Moses saw two Israelites fighting and He
        separated them;
The attacker said, 'Who made you our leader and judge?
Will you kill me as you did the Egyptian yesterday?'"
"Moses fled when he heard the accusations, realizing his actions
Were known. He fled to the land of Midian
Where he became father of two sons."
"Forty years later in the desert near Mount Sinai,
An angel appeared to him in the flames of
A burning bush and he was curious."
"As he drew closer to the bush, a voice said,
'I am the God of your ancestors,
The God of Abraham, Isaac, and Jacob.'"
"Moses trembled and couldn't look at the fire;
The LORD said, 'Take off your shoes, you
Are standing on holy ground.'"
"The LORD also said, 'I have seen the suffering of My people,
And I have heard their cries for deliverance,
And I have come down to deliver them.'"
"Come do My command, go deliver My people from Egypt."
"'This was the same Moses they rejected saying,
'Who made you our leader and judge?'"
"Now Moses was sent by God to be both leader and judge;

He performed miracles and signs in Egypt, then led them
Through the Red Sea and through the desert forty years."
"Moses told the people, 'God will raise up a prophet for you,
Like myself, from among your people.'"
"Moses was the mediator between the people and God;
He gave them the living law of God from Mount Sinai."
"But the people rejected Moses, and wanted to return to Egypt;
They asked Aaron to make idols for them so
They could have gods to lead them back to Egypt."
"They made a golden calf and offered sacrifices to it
And were happy in what they were doing."
"God gave them up and let them worship the sun
The moon, and the stars as their gods."
"In the Book of Amos, the LORD God asks,
'Were you sacrificing to Me forty years in the wilderness?'
'No! You carried the sanctuary of Moloch on your backs
You carried the star-God of Rephen in your hearts.'
'You worshiped idols that you made
So I will exile you to Babylon.'"
"While in the desert, our forefathers carried the Tabernacle
With them that Moses had them construct
From the pattern that God gave him."

Stephen continued preaching,

"It was handed down from one generation to another
Until Joshua conquered the nations and drove them out
And the Tabernacle was set up in the new territory."
"Israel worshiped in the Tabernacle until the time of David,
Then he asked for permission to build a Temple for Israel,
Though Solomon actually built the house of God."
"Even so, the Most High does not live in a house
Built by human hands, as the prophet quoted You, saying;
'Heaven is My home, the earth is My footstool,

What kind of home could you build for Me?
Didn't I make the heavens and the earth?'"

Lord, so many people are turning to sin,
   Turning from You and turning to the world.
Also, people with a hardened heart are persecuting
   The preachers that You send to call Your people back to You.
Lord, may I never be a persecutor of others.

Stephen continued preaching,
   "You are stiff-necked with a heathen heart; you are
   Resisting the Holy Spirit, just as your ancestors;
   Name one prophet your ancestors didn't persecute."
   "In the past they killed the prophets who predicted
   The coming of the Just One;
   The One you betrayed and murdered."
   "You had the Law given to you by angels, but
   You have deliberately destroyed it."

They were outraged when they heard these stinging
   Accusations against themselves.
Stephen was filled with the Holy Spirit, looked into Heaven
   And saw the glory of God and Jesus standing at God's right hand.
He said, "I see the heavens opened and the Son of Man
   Standing at the right hand of God."
But they covered their ears with their hands and furiously
   Yelled at him, and rushed at him and carried him
   Out of the city and stoned him.
They dropped their coats at the feet of a young man named Saul
   And stoned Stephen who called on God saying,
   "Lord Jesus, receive my spirit."
Then kneeling, Stephen cried out to God;
   "Lord, forgive their sin,"
   And with these words, he died and Saul approved of his death.

Amen

The Story of Saul's Rise to Power

Saul went to the Sanhedrin. He had a plan to stop the spread of Christianity. When they stoned Stephen, they had stopped the street preaching of Christians; they no longer gathered publicly for prayer. Jewish spies reported Christians were leaving Jerusalem for other cities— Alexandria, Babylon, and Damascus. They chose these cities because of the large Jewish populations there. Saul was furious,

"Christians are going to proselytize their relatives…," he announced to the Sanhedrin. Saul spoke from the back row to the assembly of 70 men. Paul was in the back row because he was not yet 30 years of age. He was a youngster among the ancient elders.

With his fist clenched, the blood vessels on his temple popped out and the tempo of his voice rose to a speedier pitch.

Paul reasoned, "We must stop the spread of Christianity…," he paused to look from face to face, they agreed. "We MUST stop them." They all nodded approval, anticipating his plan.

"I'll go to Damascus," Saul suggested, "arrest the Christians, then get a letter of extradition to bring them to Jerusalem."

"You can't do that," an old Rabbi stroked his beard to embarrass young Saul. "We have no legal rights in Damascus." Several of the older members of the Sanhedrin muttered their agreement. Another member spoke against Saul, "We have no legal authority outside the Holy Land."

"Yes we do," Saul snapped at the old man. Saul was a student of Gamaliel, which meant he did his research well before speaking. "Yes, we have legal authority…in Damascus…in Alexandria…in Babylon." Saul stopped to make his point, then continued, "We have a legal authority over Jews anywhere in the Roman Empire."

Saul explained some history to the hushed assembly. He revealed how the High Priest supported Julius Caesar in his battle to defeat Pompeii in Egypt in 68 B.C. In return, Caesar gave to Hyreanus II, the High Priest and all succeeding High Priests, spiritual authority over all Jews in the Roman Empire.

Then Saul concluded, "These Christians are Jews…legal-born Jews…." The group of men smiled at the brilliance of the young Saul. Then Saul smiled back at the Sanhedrin when he saw they were on his side. Then Saul said, "This is a spiritual matter of the highest urgency. It threatens the faith of Jews everywhere."

The group broke out into applause to show appreciation and agreement. But Saul didn't want their gratitude yet. He had one last thing to add, "We can't let the authorities in these other towns deal with these Christians. They won't stop the Christians. They won't punish them as we dealt with Stephen. We must arrest the Christian leaders, bring them back to Jerusalem, and let them feel the fury of the stones."

"YES," the Sanhedrin shouted. "Yes. Yes."

Saul had not gone to the High Priest privately with his plan for fear of rejection, rejection because he was so young. So Saul used the public platform of the Sanhedrin to intimidate the High Priest. Saul wanted the Sanhedrin to pressure the High Priest. Saul carried the day, the Sanhedrin agreed; now would the High Priest agree? All eyes looked way from Saul to the High Priest.

The room sensed tension between young Saul and the old High Priest. It was a generation gap between a young hot head and the older, wiser leader. The eyes of the Sanhedrin darted from Saul's face to the High Priest's eyes. Would the old man approve the bold initiative? He slowly opened his lips to speak,

"I will give Saul a letter of authority."

With one ingenious plan, young Saul—not yet 30 years old—became one of the leading forces in the Sanhedrin. Saul achieved authority that some members never get in a lifetime. Saul became the representative of the High Priest and a powerful voice of the Sanhedrin.

Christians Leave Jerusalem

Acts 8:1-4

Saul approved of the death of Stephen
    And immediately that day a storm of persecution
    Erupted in Jerusalem against the church
And believers fled into the countrysides of Judea and Samaria
    To escape persecution, except the apostles;
    However, some reverently buried Stephen and mourned for him.
Saul then worked feverishly to destroy all remains of the church,
    Going house to house, he dragged men and women to prison;
    Christians who were scattered went everywhere preaching the Word.

Lord, thank You for the example of martyrs who gave all in death;
    Others were willing to suffer or go to prison for You.
I'll give You everything in life, and if I have to suffer or die,
    Give me the spirit to do all for Your glory.

Philip Ministers in Samaria

Acts 8:5-25

So Philip the deacon went to Samaria to preach Christ;
    The crowds paid close attention to what Philip preached
    Because they heard about what he did and saw His miracles.
Evil spirits screamed as they were cast out of their victims
    And the paralyzed and lame were healed;
    As a result, there was great joy in the city.
A man named Simon had formerly been practicing magic
    And amazed crowds by the mystifying things he did,
    The people said, "Simon must be sent by God."
Previously, the people had listened to him because of his magic
    But Simon became a believer when Philip preached.

Many men and women were converted and baptized because of Philip
    Who preached the Kingdom of God and the name of Jesus Christ;
    Simon also was baptized because he believed.
Simon followed Philip everywhere he went
    Because he was astonished at the miracles he saw.

When the apostles in Jerusalem heard all that was happening
    In Samaria, they sent Peter and John to check it out.
Peter and John prayed for the Samaritans to receive the Holy Spirit;
    They had been baptized in the name of the Lord Jesus,
    But they had not received the Holy Spirit.

So the apostles laid hands on the people and prayed for them,
    And they received the Holy Spirit.
When Simon saw that the people received the Holy Spirit
    He wanted the same power in his hands.
So Simon offered Peter and John money saying,
    "Give me this power so I can lay hands on people
    So they can receive the Holy Spirit."
Peter erupted, "Your money will go to hell, and you with it,
    Because you think money can buy what God gives for free."
"You have no part in this ministry,
    Because your heart is not right with God."
"Turn from your wickedness and pray to God. Perhaps
    He will forgive your sin for thinking this evil."
"It is plain that you are a prisoner of greed;" Simon cried out,
    "Pray for me that nothing you said will happen to me."
The apostles preached in that city and many other Samaritan villages
    Then returned to Jerusalem.

Lord, there are some in the church who don't possess eternal life,
    They only pretend to be Christians, but they're really lost.
Help me to realize who they are, and may I help them
    Come to know You as Lord and Savior of their life.

Philip Ministers to the Ethiopian Eunuch

Acts 8:26-40

The angel of the Lord then spoke to Philip,
  "Go south to the route through the desert from Jerusalem to Gaza."
There Philip saw an important Ethiopian official who was returning
  From worshiping in Jerusalem.
This Ethiopian was the country's treasurer, who was
  Reading the Book of Isaiah out loud to his entourage
  As he rode along in his chariot.
The Holy Spirit told Philip, "Go meet this man;"
  As Philip approached, he heard the man reading from Isaiah;
  Philip asked, "Do you understand what you're reading?"
"How can I," the man answered, "unless someone helps me;"
  So the Ethiopian invited Philip to ride with him.
He was reading, "We are like sheep that are led to the slaughter,
  Like a lamb that says nothing before its shearers,
  He never opened His mouth."
"He was humiliated, but no one defended Him;
  Who will ever talk about his descendents,
  Since His life is cut short on earth?"
The Eunuch asked Philip, "Is this passage a reference
  To the prophet who wrote it, or to someone else?"
Beginning with this text, Philip explained to him
  The Good News of Jesus Christ.
A little farther they came to a pool of water. The Eunuch said,
  "Look at the water, is there any reason why I can't
  Be baptized right here, right now?"
The Eunuch ordered the chariot to stop, then the Eunuch
  And Philip went down into the water and Philip baptized him.
After they came out of the water, the Holy Spirit
  Caught away Philip. The Eunuch never saw him again,
  Then the treasurer went on his way rejoicing.

Philip found himself in Azotus, and continued preaching
   The Good News in every town until he got to Caesarea.

Lord, may I always rejoice when someone gets saved and baptized;
   Help me be a faithful witness to lost people.
Lord, there are many religious people who are blinded to the truth,
   Even as the Eunuch who didn't understand the Scriptures he read.
May I be able to help them understand Your truth,
   And lead them to a saving knowledge of Jesus Christ.

Amen

The Story of Paul's Conversion

Several weeks later, Paul was part of a caravan of camels, donkeys, and weary travelers who reached the mountain of balsam trees west of the Baca Valley. They could see Damascus in the distance from the top of the hills. Looking back they could see the cedars of Lebanon across the Baca Valley and to the south they could see Mt. Hermon, the snow-covered mountain of the Holy Land.

Saul not only had a letter from the High Priest to arrest and extradite Jews to Jerusalem, he had a letter of credit to pay his expenses. Saul was riding a horse, the most luxurious of all ways to travel. He was not being bounced on the back of a donkey, nor was he being jerked about on camel back. Rich people rode horses, as did army officers, so Saul used his letter of credit to secure a fine horse, one that called attention to the importance that he thought his new office demanded. His luggage was being brought by porters, again an opulent show of wealth. From time to time, Saul would ride out to high observation points, there he sat like a Roman Army officer surveying a battlefield. It gave Saul a sense of self-worth.

The caravan descended the green fertile hills onto the flat plain of Ghuta. Shortly, they would drink from the Barada River, then follow the river to the city of Damascus. They would enter the "East Gate" to the city. Saul planned to ride his steed triumphantly down the street called Straight that ran east and west, straight through the city. They would reach the city at high noon, the time to make the greatest entrance.

Saul's horse drank deeply in the Barada River, he paused for a rest while the caravan went before him. When he finally caught up to the caravan, his luggage handlers were walking at the rear of the caravan. It wasn't a place Saul wanted to ride for very long, he was eating the dust of the other animals.

Saul took a white cloth to wipe the perspiration from his face and neck. He tilted his head back and looked into the sun, directly into its blinding rays. The light of the sun exploded brighter than any sun Saul had ever seen. He was blinded with its brilliance, but it was not the noon sun that blinded Saul. The intense light—the light that blinded Saul—was the Lord Jesus Christ Himself.

The horse, sensing fear, began kicking wildly. Saul was not a trained horseman; he couldn't handle a kicking horse. Blinded by the searing light and losing his equilibrium, he fell to the ground. The light was so intense, Saul covered his face with both hands; sandy hands he had used to break his fall. Covering his face with his dirty hands, he couldn't look at the sun; he couldn't look at Jesus Christ. Saul couldn't see anything.

Saul was blind.

The luggage handlers saw the intense light. They dropped their burden to the ground, and cowered in fear. They didn't know what was happening, but they knew it was supernatural. They heard a voice from Heaven, it was noise to them; they couldn't make out the words. But they knew someone was speaking to Saul. A voice spoke to Saul in the Hebrew language,

"Saul...," his blinded eyes looked skyward, but were unable to see, "Saul, why are you persecuting Me?"

"Who are You?" Saul stammered an answer.

"I am Jesus...," the voice from Heaven answered. "You think you are persecuting Christians, but you are persecuting Me."

Saul quickly processed everything in his mind. He hated Christians and was willing to kill them, just as other Jewish leaders killed Jesus. He knew Christians claimed Jesus was not dead, but was alive. Now Jesus was talking to him. Saul heard the voice,

"I am Jesus…it is hard to kick against the truth." Saul lay groveling in the dirt, thrown by a kicking horse. Instantly, Saul knew his whole legalistic approach to God was wrong. Christians didn't just have a better system of religion, they believed in a person. They followed Christ. Saul answered,

"Lord…," it was the first time Saul acknowledged the deity of Jesus Christ. "Lord…, what do you want me to do?"

In that statement, Saul yielded himself to a person. It would take awhile to sort out his theology, and he would have to think his way through all the changes that would be required in his lifestyle. But lying on the ground, Saul made one monumental change—he recognized the person of Jesus Christ. Even though blinded, Saul had seen the light. Even though blinded by the light, Saul had seen the brilliance of Jesus Christ. In yieldedness, Saul asked,

"What do you want me to do?"

The Lord gave him instructions, "Arise," Saul was to get up off the ground. "Get up, go into the city; you will be told what to do."

The horse had run away, the luggage carriers didn't go after it for the horse was not their concern. They had seen the blinding light and heard a voice speaking from Heaven. Now working for a blinded employer, they had to get him to the city if they wanted their money. The city gate was right ahead. Taking Saul by the arm, they led him on the street called Straight, to a house of a Jewish man named Judah. What a spectacle, Saul did not have a triumphant entrance upon a fine white horse. Saul was being led by his luggage handlers, he had blinded eyes and dirty robes—God had humbled Saul.

Saul was ugly, because his eyes were ugly. Not only was he blinded, but also rubbing sand into his eyes had irritated them and bloodied them.

The more he tried to open his eyes, the more intense his pain, like needles piercing his eyeballs. Any light was unbearable. Saul squeezed them to shut out any light, then rubbed them until they bled. The more his eyes bled, the more Saul rubbed them creating huge ugly blood-crusted scabs in place of eyes. Saul had been spiritually blind, now he was also physically blind.

The Conversion of Saul

Acts 9:1-19

Meanwhile, Saul was still threatening to destroy every Christian;
  He had a letter from the High Priest that gave him authority
  To arrest Christians in Damascus and bring them to Jerusalem.
Suddenly, as he almost reached Damascus, a blinding light
  From Heaven shone all about him.
Saul fell to the ground and heard a voice saying,
  "Saul, Saul, why are you persecuting Me?"
Saul answered, "Who are you, Lord?" The voice answered,
  "I am Jesus whom you are persecuting."
"Now get up and go into the city, and
  You will be told what you must do."
The men traveling with Saul stood speechless.
  They heard the sound, but didn't see anyone.
Saul got up from the ground, but when he opened his eyes,
  He could see nothing. He was blind,
  So they led him into the city of Damascus.
There he remained blind for three days;
  During that time, he ate and drank nothing.

Lord, I've met You and was saved. While my conversion
  Was not as dramatic as Saul's, I nevertheless know You are real;
I once was blind in my sin, but now I see.

In Damascus there was a follower of Christ named Ananias.
>   The Lord called him by name in a dream. He responded,
>   "Here am I, Lord."
"Go to the street called Straight" the Lord said, "to the
>   House of Judah and ask for Saul from Tarsus. He is
>   Praying. Saul knows you are coming
>   To lay hands upon his eyes to restore his sight."
But Ananias replied, "Lord, I have heard evil reports
>   About this man. He has done terrible things to Your servants;
>   He has come with authority to arrest those who call on Your name."
The Lord said to Ananias, "Go pray for him, because I have chosen
>   Saul as an instrument to preach My name before Gentiles and Kings
>   And he will suffer much for My name's sake."
So Ananias found Saul, and laid hands on him, and said, "Brother
>   Saul, the Lord Jesus who appeared to you on the road sent me
>   So you will be filled with the Holy Spirit and get your sight back."
Instantly, the scales fell from his eyes and Saul could see;
>   Then he was baptized, and ate and was strengthened;
>   Saul stayed with Christians in Damascus for a while.

Lord, Saul began serving You immediately after he was saved,
>   *Help me be diligent in serving You, as did Saul.*
Lead me today to people and places where I can serve You,
>   *I want to be busy in the work of Your Kingdom.*

Saul Begins Preaching the Gospel

Acts 9:20-31

Immediately Saul went to the Synagogues to preach the Good News
>   That Jesus was indeed the Son of God.
All who heard Saul were amazed, and asked, "Isn't this the man
>   Who arrested Christians in Jerusalem
>   And came here to do the same thing?"

Saul became more fervent in preaching;
> The Damascus Synagogue was silenced
> By the strength of Saul's preaching that Jesus was the Christ.

After a time, the Jews plotted to kill Saul, but he heard about it;
> The assassins waited at the gate night and day, but at night the
> Believers helped Saul escape over the wall in a basket.

When Saul got to Jerusalem, he tried to join the Christians
> But they were afraid of him.
> They were not sure Saul was a true believer.

Barnabas received Saul and introduced him to the apostles,
> And explained how the Lord appeared to Saul, and
> What the Lord had said to him, and how Saul had preached
> In the name of Jesus boldly in the Synagogue in Damascus.

Then the believers accepted Saul and he preached boldly among them,
> Some Greek-speaking Jews to whom Saul preached
> Then plotted to murder him.

The believers heard about it and took Saul to Caesarea,
> And then sent him to his hometown in Tarsus.

Lord, although the church was no longer threatened by persecution;
> They grew in number, and spiritual maturity.

They no longer worried about persecution, but they feared You
> Because the Holy Spirit was their Comforter.

Lord, help me to be a persistent witness to You
> *Even when people refuse to believe and reject my message.*
May opposition make me stronger in my faith, and
> *More determined to serve You.*

Amen

Ministry of Peter

Acts 9:32-43

Lord, Peter was traveling to evangelize the lost
> And encourage the churches. When he came to Lydda,

He found Aeneas who had been paralyzed eight years.
Peter said, "Aeneas, Jesus Christ heals you, get up; and
    Fold your mat." He was healed instantly.
Everyone living in the area turned to the Lord
    When they saw Aeneas walking.

A woman named Dorcas who lived in Joppa, died;
    She was a believer who always did kind things for
    Others, especially the poor. Her friends prepared the body
    For burial and placed it in an upstairs room.
When the people learned Peter was nearby, they sent two men
    To bring him to Joppa. When Peter arrived,
    He went upstairs to where Dorcas lay.
The room was filled with widows who showed Peter
    The clothes Dorcas had made for them. Peter
    Sent them out of the room, and knelt to pray.
Peter turned to the dead body and said, "Tabitha, stand up;"
    She opened her eyes, looked at Peter, and sat up;
    Peter helped her to her feet and presented her to the believers.
When the people of Joppa heard of the miracle,
    Many of them believed in the Lord.
Peter stayed there for some time,
    Living with Simon, the Tanner.

Lord, I know You can do all things, I praise You
    That You hold life and health in Your hands.
Give me faith to trust You to do miracles;
    When I don't know how to pray, teach me how,
    And show me the things for which I must pray.

Amen

God Sends a Message to Cornelius

Acts 10:1-8

A captain named Cornelius in the Italian regiment
>   of the Roman Army was stationed at the military fortress in
>   Caesare.

He was a religious man who led his whole family
>   To worship God, give to the poor and prayed constantly.

About 3:00 P.M. Cornelius saw an angel come to him in a vision
>   As he stared at the angel in fear, Cornelius said,
>   "What do you want with me?"

The angel answered, "God has heard your prayers, and seen
>   Your works for the poor, so now He will answer you."

"Send some men to Joppa to get Simon Peter,
>   Who is a guest in the home of Simon the Tanner,
>   Who lives by the sea."

When the angel went away, Cornelius told what happened to two
>   Of his servants and a soldier who was religious;
>   He then sent them to Joppa to get Peter.

Lord, I'm glad You have compassion on extremely religious people
>   *Who seek You, but have never heard the Gospel.*

Thank You for making a way for people like Cornelius to hear the Gospel;
>   *I pray for the billions of unsaved who have never heard,*
>   *Stir their hearts to seek salvation in Christ, as you did Cornelius.*

Peter's Vision and His Response

Acts 10:9-23

As they approached Joppa the next day about noon, Peter
>   Was praying up on the roof top while the others were
>   Preparing lunch; Peter was ready to eat.

It was then Peter had a vision where he saw Heaven opened
    And a large sheet being lowered by the four corners.
In it were all kinds of animals, reptiles and wild birds;
    He heard a voice say, "Get up, Peter, kill and eat."
Peter answered, "I can't do that Lord."
    "I have never eaten anything that was unclean or defiled."
The voice spoke again, "Do not call anything unclean
    That God has cleansed." This happened three times,
    Then the sheet was taken back to Heaven.
As Peter was thinking about what just happened,
    The men sent by Cornelius arrived at the gate to the house.
They called out, "Is there a guest here by the name of Simon Peter?"
    Peter was still trying to understand what he saw
    When the Spirit of God said, "Three men are looking for you."
"Do not hesitate to go with them for I have sent them;"
    Then Peter went down and told them, "I am Peter,
    Why have you come looking for me?"
They told Peter, "Our leader, Cornelius, sent us to invite you
    To come to his house so he could hear what you have to say."
They also told Peter that Cornelius was a good man, who
    Worshiped God, and the Jewish people respected him.
Peter invited the men into the house,
    And they stayed the night with Peter.

Lord, I'm grateful for those who go to the billions who have never heard,
    Some go to dangerous situations, some give up riches and positions.
Bless those who preach the Gospel to those who have never heard,
    May many hear and believe and be saved.
Lord, I'm willing to go where You send me, and I'm willing to do
    Anything You want me to do, just guide me today.

Amen

Peter and Cornelius Exchange Greetings

Acts 10:24-33

The following day Peter arrived in Caesarea at Cornelius' house
>   Where he was waiting for Peter with all his relations and
>   friends.

As Peter was about to enter, Cornelius met him and
>   Bowed at his feet saying he was unworthy to receive Peter.

But Peter made him rise saying, "Stand up, I am only a man;"
>   And Peter went inside with Cornelius, where he found a crowd
>   And said, "You know that a Jew can't associate with Gentiles."

Peter explained, "God has shown me that
>   I must not consider any person ritually unclean or defiled."

"Therefore, I came without objection.
>   Now, why did you send for me?"

Cornelius explained, "About this time three days ago
>   I was praying in my house when suddenly
>   A man in shining garments appeared to me, saying,

'God has heard your prayers, and seen your charity, send
>   Your servants to Joppa for a man named Peter,
>   He is a guest at the home of Simon a Tanner.'"

"So I sent for you at once—thank you for coming;
>   Now we are all here in the presence of God
>   Waiting to hear anything God has told you to say to us."

Lord, there are many who are hungry to hear the Good News,
>   *May I always be willing and ready to tell them about Jesus.*

Amen

Peter's Sermon in Cornelius' Home

Acts 10:34-43

Then Peter spoke to the gathering, "God does not play favorites
But He accepts people from any nation who do the right things."
"God sent His message of peace through Jesus Christ to Israel
Because Jesus is Lord of all."
"You know what happened throughout Judea, beginning in Galilee,
After the Baptism of John, how God anointed Jesus of Nazareth
With the Holy Spirit and power,
"He went about doing good, healing all under the devil's power,
Because God was with Him."
"We are witnesses of everything Jesus did in Judea and Jerusalem,
And we saw they killed Him by hanging Jesus on a tree."
"Yet three days later God raised Him from the dead,
And He was seen by witnesses God had chosen."
"Now we are those witnesses, we have eaten and drank with Him,
After He was raised from the dead."
"Now God has commanded us to tell people everywhere,
That He has appointed Jesus to judge everyone, alive or dead,
And the prophets witness to this fact, that all who believe in Jesus
Will have their sin forgiven through His name."

Lord, remind me how simple is the plan of salvation;
People only have to believe in Jesus to be saved.
I praise You that Peter went to people of different cultures and customs;
May I always be willing to share the Gospel with all people,
No matter if they are different from me or not.

Amen

Gentiles Are Baptized With the Holy Spirit and Water

Acts 10:44-48

While Peter was speaking, the Holy Spirit was poured out
    On those who were listening to Peter's sermon.
The Jewish Christians who came with Peter were astonished
    That the Holy Spirit was poured out on Gentiles
    Because they were speaking in unknown languages and praising God.
Peter said, "Can anyone refuse water baptism to these
    Who have received the Holy Spirit just as we did on Pentecost?"
He then gave instructions to baptize them in the name of Jesus Christ;
    Cornelius asked Peter to stay a few days.

Lord, I want the Holy Spirit to fill me with His presence;
    I want Your power and joy in my life and service.
May I never be scared or intimidated by unsaved people,
    May I always be open to the Holy Spirit and His blessing.

Amen

Peter Explains His Actions to the Jerusalem Church

Acts 11:1-18

The apostles and brethren in Judea were critical when they heard
    That Gentiles had accepted the Word of God and been baptized.
When Peter visited Jerusalem, those who still demanded circumcision
    Were critical because Peter visited and ate with Gentiles.
Peter gave them the whole background of how it happened;
    He said, "I was praying in Joppa when I had a vision
Of a big sheet let down from Heaven by its four corners;
    I saw in it all types of beasts, reptiles, and birds,
Then I heard a voice from Heaven, 'Get up Peter, kill and eat;'
    But I answered, 'I can't do that Lord, I have never

Eaten anything that was unclean or defiled.'"
"Then I heard the voice a second time saying, 'Do not call anything
    Unclean that God has cleansed.' This happened three times
    Then the sheet was taken back to Heaven."
"Just as that happened, three men sent by Cornelius arrived at the gate;
    They said they were sent from Caesarea to get me,
    The Holy Spirit told me not to hesitate to go with them."
Then Peter explained, "These six brothers standing here went with me
    And we went into Cornelius' home."
"He told us that he had seen an angel when he was praying
    That told him 'Send to Joppa to get Simon Peter
    Who will give you a message that will save you and your
        household.'"
Peter continued, "While I was preaching the Holy Spirit fell on them,
    As it had fallen on us at Pentecost."
"Then I remembered the promise of Jesus, 'John indeed baptized with
    Water, but you will be baptized by the Holy Spirit.'"
"Since God has done for Gentiles the exact same gift
    He did for us when we believed on Him,
    Who was I to stand in God's way of doing things?"
Peter's explanation satisfied them and they glorified God;
    They concluded, "Evidently, God has given to the Gentiles,
    Repentance to eternal life."

Lord, I'm grateful when Christians work out their misunderstandings;
    I'm especially thankful when they listen to one another
    Before criticizing them.
Give me patience when I disagree with others and help me
    Listen to people before I criticize them.

Amen

The Story of the Antioch Church

Barnabas stood on the Amanus Mountain range overlooking the ancient Syrian city of Antioch. From his vantage point he could see the small winding Orontes River as it made its way down to the Mediterranean Sea.

Antioch was a massive city of 800,000 people. It was called the crossroads of the Roman Empire. Huge camel trains trudged the desert sands from the East and the Euphrates River, crossing the black Ural Mountains, bringing Persian silk, spices, and all of the products that sophisticated Romans wanted. After the camel train arrived in Antioch, the goods were transferred into Roman galleons that spread out over the Mediterranean world bringing Eastern goods to Athens, Rome, Carthage, Alexandria, and the other civilized cities of the Roman Empire.

Just about every ethnic group of people was located in Antioch. Travelers got stuck there all the time, and since money was to be made, they stayed and settled down.

News of a church in Antioch got back to Jerusalem. Since there was not a Synagogue in Antioch, many wondered if there could be a church without Jews as its foundation. Many wondered what kind of mixed up group of people this could be who called themselves "Christians."

James, the leading elder in Jerusalem decided, "I'll send Barnabas to check out this group." James gave specific orders to find out if the new church believed the right things, and were they living the right way, and did they really understand the forgiveness of sins that Jesus offered to the world.

"How did they become Christians?" was a natural question that Barnabas asked.

"We don't know, but some claim to be converted on the day of Pentecost, when the Holy Spirit fell on us. Some were from Antioch. They went home and began telling others about Jesus, the Messiah."

James added a warning, "The young church in Antioch has many non-Jews who are believing; these are uncircumcised people who have put their trust in Jesus Christ." James was not sure if they understood the foundations of the faith that come from a Jewish understanding of the Old Testament.

James had a specific reason for sending Barnabas. James remembered that Barnabas had sold all the land he possessed and gave the money to the church. The property was in Cyprus and James responded that Barnabas had been to Antioch on many occasions. Most people went to Cyprus by boat from Antioch; it was approximately 60 miles by water.

When Barnabas arrived at Antioch, he sat on a hill overlooking the city, wondering, "What kind of a church will I see; what kind of Christians will I meet; what will happen to me?"

It only took Barnabas two or three days to size up the church in Antioch. The Christians represented almost every ethnic group—there were Synthians, Arabs, Greeks, Turks, and Europeans, all believed in Jesus Christ, and none of them were circumcised according to Jewish law.

The more Barnabas talked to the believers, the more he realized that they needed grounding in the Old Testament Scriptures. Barnabas was an exhorter; his primary spiritual gift was motivating people to serve God. The church in Antioch already served God. They didn't need him, they needed solid teaching.

It was then when Barnabas thought of Paul. A few years earlier when Saul, the hated persecutor of the Jews had come to Jerusalem, no one would believe that he had been converted. Many Christians were afraid that Saul's conversion was a trick so he could infiltrate the church and arrest them.

But Barnabas understood rejection. He was the rich young ruler who rejected Jesus Christ. So Barnabas went to Saul and determined that he really was saved, Saul was "pure gold." It was then when Barnabas took Saul and introduced him to James and Peter.

So, it was only natural for Barnabas to be sent to this young "rejected" church in Antioch to find out if they were "pure gold."

Barnabas thought, "Saul is a teacher trained in the law who knows the Word of God." It was then when Barnabas determined to travel some 150 miles overland to Tarsus in Asia Minor to Saul's home. Saul had been ministering to his people when he left Jerusalem.

The journey to Tarsus took a week, but it only took a few minutes for Barnabas to convince Saul to return with him to teach the Word of God to the young Christians at Antioch.

While in Tarsus, Barnabas met some of the young converts from the university that Paul had led to Christ. Most notable among them was a medical student named Luke. Paul had some problems with asthma and Luke had been treating him. When Luke gave medical permission for Paul to leave, it was only a day later they left for Antioch.

For the next year, Paul gave the young church at Antioch a full Bible education. Beginning at Moses and the first five books of the Bible, he surveyed the foundations of the Hebrew faith. Then Paul taught them what each of the prophets believed. Finally, covering the Psalms and the historical books, the Christians in Antioch learned the Word of God completely, memorizing many of its great texts.

Barnabas said, "I can almost see Christians growing spiritually, night by night, as Saul explained the Word of God." After a year of Bible study, Barnabas observed, "The Christians here in Antioch are as strong as I've seen back in Jerusalem." Barnabas realized that this was a strong church that could do much to carry out the Great Commission in all the world.

The Church at Antioch

Acts 11:19-26

Those who fled Jerusalem when Saul persecuted Christians
     Had traveled as far as Phoenicia, Cyprus, and Antioch.
At Antioch, they shared the Gospel with Greeks,
     Giving the Good News of Jesus Christ to them as well as Jews;
     God worked powerfully and a large number of Gentiles
     Turned to the Lord.
When this news reached the church in Jerusalem,

They sent Barnabas to check out the church in Antioch;
    Barnabas was a good man, full of the Holy Spirit and Faith.
When Barnabas arrived, he saw what God was doing and rejoiced;
    Then he encouraged them to be strong in the faith;
    As a result, a number of people became Christians.
Then Barnabas went to Tarsus to find Saul, and brought
    Saul back to Antioch where he taught the believers for a year;
    In Antioch believers were first called Christians.

Lord, I rejoice when the Gospel is spread
    To places where people don't know You.
May I do all I can to help plant new churches,
    To evangelize areas that need the good news.

Amen

Help for the Jerusalem Church

Acts 11:27-30

Some prophets came down to Antioch from Jerusalem; one of them,
    Agabus, predicted that a great famine was coming
    Before the end of the reign of Claudius.
The believers at Antioch decided to send supplies to the church in
    Jerusalem
    So each believer gave what they could afford;
    Barnabas and Saul delivered the supplies to Jerusalem.

Lord, You have given to Your followers a spirit of Charity;
    Thank You for those who gave to me when I was in need.
Now, I determine to give to those in need. I will give what I can give;
    I will be charitable and giving with what You give me.

Amen

James Killed—Peter Imprisoned

Acts 12:1-17

About this time King Herod began persecuting the church in Jerusalem,
>He had James, the brother of John, put to death with the sword;
>When he saw it pleased the Jews, he arrested Peter.

He imprisoned Peter because it was the high feast of Passover, and Herod
>Intended to bring Peter to trial after Passover.

Peter was guarded by four squads of four soldiers;
>As Peter was in prison, the church prayed earnestly for him.

Peter was chained to two soldiers, sleeping between them;
>And there were two guards at the entrance.

Suddenly, there was a light in the cell and an angel stood next to Peter,
>He had to shake Peter to awaken him;
>The angel said, "Get up quickly," and the chains fell off Peter.

Then the angel said, "Get dressed—don't forget your shoes—
>And follow me." Peter thought it was a dream,
>And he didn't believe it was happening.

They passed the first and second cell, then came to the iron gate
>That led to the city. It opened by itself.

They walked out into the street, and as they were walking,
>The angel disappeared. Finally Peter realized, "This is happening!"

"The Lord has sent an angel to rescue me from Herod
>And all that the Jewish leaders wanted to do to me."

Peter went to the home of Mary, the mother of John Mark,
>Where Christians had gathered to pray for him.

When Peter knocked at the outer gate, Rhoda, a servant girl,
>Looked out and recognized him. She got so excited she
>Didn't open the gate, but ran to tell everyone.

They said, "You're out of your mind," but Rhoda kept saying
>Peter was at the gate. They thought Peter had been executed
>And that his angel was at the gate.

Peter kept knocking, and when they opened the gate,
    They were amazed that it was really Peter.
Peter raised his hand to stop their talking, then he told them
    How the Lord had led him out of the prison.
Peter instructed them to tell James the Lord's brother and others,
    Then he went to a place where Herod couldn't find him.
At dawn, there was a great commotion at the jail over
    The disappearance of Peter. They searched thoroughly for Peter
    And when he couldn't be found, Herod ordered the guards executed.

Lord, some of your servants are martyred like James
    If that's my lot, have Your way in my life.
Lord, if you deliver me from persecution, like Peter,
    I'll praise You for an easy life;
    May I always serve You, no matter what happens to me.

Amen

Herod Judged

Acts 12:18-25

Herod lived at Caesarea in the summer time. While there the
    People of Tyre and Sidon sought an audience with the king
    Because there was a quarrel between them and Herod.
Blastus, a trusted servant of Herod, worked out a compromise
    Because the people needed Herod's permission for their food supply.
When the day came for the people to meet Herod, he delivered an address
    To them wearing his crown and royal regalia.
The people shouted, "This is the voice of god, not of man,"
    And they gave him a rousing ovation.
Instantly, an angel from God struck him with a disease,
    And he was filled with maggots and died—

Because he accepted the people's worship instead of giving it
to God.

The Good News was spreading rapidly and many people were saved;
Barnabas and Saul returned from Jerusalem when they finished
Their ministry and returned to Antioch,
Taking John Mark with them.

Lord, what a terrible sin for anyone to receive Your worship;
Help me deal properly with pride and give You glory for everything.
I want to be more godly and I want to walk humbly with You;
Help me say with believers, "Not I, but Christ."

Amen

God Called Barnabas and Saul to be Missionaries

Acts 13:1-3

The church at Antioch had prophets and teachers: Barnabas,
Simeon called Niger, Lucius of Cyrene, Manaen,
Who was raised with Herod, and Saul.
While they were worshiping God and fasting, the Holy Spirit said,
"Send Barnabas and Saul to a special ministry,
To which I have called them."
So after more fasting and prayer, they laid their hands on them,
And sent them out to minister.

Lord, teach me to listen to Your voice for direction to my life,
Just as the leaders in Antioch sought Your will for their life and
ministry.
I will seek Your will in my life. When You speak
Give me ears to hear what You want me to do
And give me strength to choose to do Your will.

Amen

Ministry in Cyprus

Acts 13:4-12

These two men—sent by the Holy Spirit—went to Selucia,
     And sailed to the island of Cyprus.
When they landed in Salamis, they preached the Word of the Lord
     In the Synagogue of the Jews. John went along to look after details.
They traveled the whole length of the island, and came in contact
     With a Jewish magician named Bar-Jesus.
This false prophet was an attendant of Sergius Paulus,
     The Roman governor of the island, who was extremely intelligent.
The governor called for Barnabas and Saul because he wanted to hear
     The Word of God. The Jewish magician, Elymas Magos,
     The Greek name for Bar-Jesus,
Tried to stop Barnabas and Saul because it looked like the governor
     Would be converted to the Christian faith.
Saul, whose name was changed to Paul at this time,
     Was filled with the Holy Spirit to stop the magician;
     Paul stared angrily at him and said,
"You son of the devil…you enemy of God…you are opposing God,
     Now God's hand will judge you, you will be blind!"
Instantly his eyes became misty and then everything went dark;
     He groped about, seeking someone to lead him by the hand.
The governor who was watching became a believer, for he was
     Astonished by what he saw and what he heard.

Lord, I want to be as courageous in witnessing for You
     As Paul was when he boldly faced opposition.
Teach me how to react when people oppose me for my faith;
     I want to react properly to attacks and I want people
     To get saved, as the governor was converted.

Amen

Ministry in Turkey

Acts 13:13-52

Paul and his companions sailed from Paphos to Pergia in modern day
Turkey,
Here John Mark left them to go back home to Jerusalem;
They went from Pergia to Antioch of Pisidia.
On the Sabbath day they went to the Synagogue and took a seat;
After the lesson from the Law and the prophets were read,
The president of the Synagogue asked Paul,
"Would you like to give some words of encouragement to the congregation?"
Paul stood, held up his hand for silence, then spoke,
"Listen, men of Israel and you Gentiles who worship the God of our
nation Israel,
God chose us and made us a large nation when we lived
As foreigners in Egypt. Then by supernatural power,
God led Israel out of Egypt, and took care of them
For 40 years in the wilderness; then God destroyed seven nations
As He put Israel in the Holy Land as their inheritance.
They lived there 450 years."
"After that God gave them judges until the coming of the prophet Samuel;
When our people begged for a king, God gave them Saul,
Of the tribe of Benjamin. He was their king for 40 years."
"After God disposed of Saul, He raised up David to the throne
Whom God Himself said, 'A man after My own heart,
Who shall do all My will.'"

"To keep His promise, God brought forth Jesus from the descendents of
David
To be the Savior of Israel."
"John the Baptist came before Him to prepare the way of Jesus,
Preaching the baptism of repentance for all the people of Israel."
"John said, 'I am not the Messiah, but the One coming

After Me is so great, I'm not fit to loose his shoe strings.'"
"Saul preached, 'Men and brethren, Sons of Abraham, and
      Gentiles who fear God, God has sent you this message of salvation.'
"The people of Jerusalem and their leaders refused to recognize Jesus
      Even though they read the prophets every Sabbath day
      That predicts His coming as Messiah."
"Even though there was nothing to justify the death of Jesus,
      They asked Pilate to execute Him."
"When they did everything to Jesus that the Scriptures foretold,
      They took Him down from the tree and buried Him in a tomb."
"But God raised Jesus up from the dead, and for many days
      He appeared to His followers from Galilee,
      These are now His witnesses before the world."

"We have come here to tell you the Good News. God made the promises
      To our ancestors, but it is to us—their children—
That He has fulfilled these promises by raising Jesus from the dead;
      As the psalms say, 'You are my Son, today I have become Your
           Father.'
"This Psalm means that God raised Jesus from the dead,
      Never to return to corruption."
"God has given to Jesus the wonderful things
      He promised David, 'He will not let his Holy One decay.'"
"This was not a reference to David because after he lived seventy years,
      And served his generation, David died and his body decayed."
"This was a reference to another person whom God
      Brought back to life, whose body was not touched
      By the ravages of death. This was a reference to Jesus."
"Brothers, listen, there is forgiveness for your sins in this man Jesus;
      Everyone who trusts in Him is free from all guilt,
      He will declare you righteous, something the Law cannot do."
"Be careful brothers, because the words of the prophets apply to you,
      Cast your eyes around you mockers,
      Be amazed before you perish,

For I work a work in your days,
A work that you absolutely will not believe
If you were to be told of it."

As Paul and Barnabas left, many Jews and Gentile converts insisted
They return the next Sabbath to speak on this topic.

Lord, help me realize many people are hungry for the Good News
That Jesus forgives sins, gives eternal life, and gives abundant
Satisfaction.

The next Sabbath, almost the whole city assembled to hear
The Word of the Lord. When the Jews saw the multitude,
They were envious, and debated the things Paul said.
Then Paul and Barnabas boldly answered them,
"It was our duty to speak the Good News to you Jews
Who have demonstrated yourselves unworthy of eternal life."
"So now we are turning to the Gentiles, as the Lord has instructed us to do;
'I have set you as a light to the Gentiles
So my salvation will reach to the end of the earth.'"

The Gentiles were glad to hear this message, and
Thanked God for it. Many of them believed.
The Word of the Lord spread throughout the region,
But the Jews stirred up the women and civic leaders
Against Paul and Barnabas, and threw them out of town.
But the missionaries shook the dust of that town off their feet
And went to the next city of Iconium;
The converts were filled with joy and the Holy Spirit.

Lord, thank You for the spread of the Gospel to those
Who have never heard, and thank You for new converts.
If Paul and Barnabas had not gone with the Gospel
To the Gentiles, I would not be converted today.

Amen

In Antioch

Acts 14:1-6

At Iconium, Paul and Barnabas went into the Jewish Synagogue
 As they did in Antioch and spoke so effectively
 That a great number of Jews became followers of Jesus Christ.
But the Jews who refused to believe, stirred up the Gentiles against them
 But Paul and Barnabas stayed there to preach fearlessly.
The Lord confirmed the message of grace and allowed
 Signs and wonders to be done by them.
The people of the city were divided, some siding with the apostles,
 Others supported the Jews. But a conspiracy was
 Made by the unbelievers to stone them.
Paul and Barnabas heard their plot and left for safety reasons;
 Leaving, they preached the Gospel in Lystra and Derbe in the
 surrounding Mountains.

Lord, thank You for every missionary who has gone
 To dangerous places to preach the Gospel.
Give me courage to stand against criticism and ridicule
 When I share the Gospel.

Amen

In Derbe and Lystra

Acts 14:7-18

A man crippled from birth sat at the city gate listening to Paul;
 Paul saw him and realized he had faith to be healed.
Then Paul said in a loud voice, "Stand up straight on your feet!"
 The man jumped up and began to walk.
When the crowd saw what happened, they shouted in their language,
 "The gods have come down to us dressed like men."

They called Barnabas Zeus, and Paul they called Hermes
  Since he was the spokesman.
The priest of Jupiter, whose temple was outside the gate
  Brought oxen and flowers to sacrifice to
  Paul and Barnabas at the city gate in front of the crowd.
But Paul and Barnabas ripped their clothes and ran into the crowd,
  Shouting, "Friends, why are you doing this?"
  "We are human beings with feelings just as you."
"We are here to tell you the good news that you
  Should turn from idols to the living God
  Who made Heaven and earth, and the sea and everything in it."
  "In the past, he let the nations go their own way,
  But there was always a witness to them;
  The earth, Heaven and the seas."
  "He sent rain giving you crops and food to eat."
This speech barely restrained the crowd from
  Offering sacrifices to them.

The Stoning of Paul

Acts 14:19-28

Then Jews arrived from Antioch and Iconium and turned the people
  Against the apostles. They stoned Paul and dragged him
  Outside the city, thinking he was dead.
The Christians gathered around him, but as they did,
  Paul stood up and went back into the town;
  The next day, Paul and Barnabas departed to Derbe.

Lord, thank You that Paul was faithful to death;
  Give me courage to face death if it ever comes my way.
Thank You that Timothy became a follower because of this experience;
  May this story of Paul strengthen the faith of many.

The next day Paul and Barnabas departed for Derbe;
>They preached the Gospel and many became Christians.
They turned back and revisited Lystra, Iconium, and Antioch of Turkey
>Where they strengthened the disciples of Christ in those cities,
>Exhorting them to be strong in the faith and endure many
>>tribulations.
After prayer and fasting, they appointed church leaders in every church
>Commending these men to the Lord for their new ministry.
They then crossed over the mountains to Pisidia, going to Pamphylia;
>After preaching the Word of God in Pergia, they went
>To Attalia and then sailed back to Antioch of Syria.
They arrived back at the church that originally commissioned them
>Because they had completed the work they intended to do.
They assembled the church together and reported all that God had done
Especially how He had opened the door of faith to the Gentiles;
>They stayed in Antioch a long time.

Lord, I thank You for every missionary who has gone to unreached
>*Places to preach the Gospel to those who have never head it.*
Thank You for those who brought the Gospel to my nation and my people;
>*Please call more missionaries so every place and*
>*Ethnic group on earth can hear the Gospel at least once.*

Amen

The First Church Council

Acts 15:1-41

Some men came to Antioch from Judaea teaching,
>"You are not saved unless you have been circumcised
>According to the practice of Moses."
A long fierce argument broke out between Paul and Barnabas
>And those who wanted to add "good works" to salvation.

It was arranged for Paul, Barnabas, and others to go to Jerusalem
>To discuss this issue with the apostles and elders.
The church gathered to see them off, and they traveled through
>Lebanon and Samaria telling how Gentiles were saved;
>Christians everywhere rejoiced when they heard this.
They were welcomed in Jerusalem by the apostles, elders, and the church,
>And they told them what God had done among the Gentiles.
Some of the converted Pharisees came forward to say the Gentiles
>Must be circumcised and keep the Law of Moses.
The apostles and elders called a meeting to discuss the issues,
>And after a long debate; Peter stood to address the council.
"My friends," he said, "you remember God chose me to preach
>The Gospel to the Gentiles at Cornelius' house so they
>>could believe."
>"God knows who is genuinely converted,
>So He gave them the Holy Spirit, just as He gave to us."
>"God made no distinction between Jew and Gentile, because
>He forgave them by faith, just as He did for us."
>"Now we are trying to correct God and impose on the Gentiles
>A burden that we nor our fathers were able to obey;
>No one has ever kept the law to be saved."
>"We are saved the same way Gentiles are saved,
>Through faith in our Lord Jesus Christ."
Peter's argument silenced the assembly, no one could say anything;
>Then Paul and Barnabas described all the signs and miracles
>God had done though them among the Gentiles.

Finally, James concluded what was said, "My brothers,
>Simon Peter has described how God worked to call to Himself
>Those who were saved among the Gentiles."
"This agrees with the words of the prophets, since the Scriptures say,
>'After that I will return and rebuild the
>Fallen house of David.'
>'I shall rebuild it from its ruins and restore it;

Then the rest of the world—the Gentiles—
    May seek the Lord to be saved.'"
James stated, "The Lord said this long ago,"
    So he ruled that they should not make
    Things more difficult for Gentiles to be saved.
James proposed they send a letter telling Gentile Christians,
    "To abstain from anything polluted by idols
    From fornication, from meat of strangled animals and blood."
James reasoned, "Because there are disciples of Moses in every place,
    They read Moses every week and faithfully obey him."

Then the apostles and elders decided to choose and send delegates
    To Antioch with Paul and Barnabas to read this letter to them.
They chose Judas known as Barnabas, and Silas;
    Both men were leaders in the Jerusalem church.
"The apostles and elders, your brothers in Christ, send greetings
    To the Gentile brothers in Antioch, Syria, and Cilicia."
    "We have heard that some of our members have upset you
    By demanding that you all be circumcised to be saved."
    "They did not have our authorization, so we have
    Unanimously elected these delegates to go with
    Paul and Barnabas to deliver this letter to you."
    "We respect highly Paul and Barnabas who have risked
    Their lives for the name of the Lord Jesus Christ."
    "Therefore we are sending Judas and Silas who will re-enforce
    What this letter says,
    The Holy Spirit has led us to conclude
    Not to burden Gentile believers with keeping the Law,
    But we want you to abstain from food sacrificed to idols,
    From blood, and the meat of strangled animals and from fornication;
    You will do right to avoid them."
    'Farewell.'"

The group left and went to Antioch where they gathered the church
  And delivered the letter to them. The church read it
  And was delighted with its conclusions.
Judas and Silas stayed preaching to the Christians in Antioch
  Then the church sent them back to their homes in Jerusalem.
Paul and Barnabas stayed in Antioch to help
  The others who were preaching and teaching to the church.
Paul said to Barnabas, "Let's go back to visit the churches
  We planted where we preached the Word of God
  So we can see how they are doing."
Barnabas wanted to take John Mark with them, but Paul
  Was not in favor of it because he had deserted
  Them in Pamphylia and refused to go on with them.
Because they disagreed, they parted ways;
  Barnabas took John Mark with him to Cyprus.
Paul chose Silas to go with him
  And the church commended them to God;
  They traveled through Syria and Turkey visiting the churches.

Paul Recruits Timothy

Acts 16:1-8

When Paul and Silas reached Derbe and Lystra, they met Timothy
  Whose mother was a Jewess but his father was a Greek.
Because Timothy was an outstanding Christian, the church
  recommended him
  To travel with Paul and Barnabas, but Paul had him circumcised
  Because of the Jews who knew his father was a Greek.

Lord, thank You for the faithfulness of Timothy;
  May I have a good testimony
  So that the church would recommend me for Your work.

Amen

The Spirit Guides Their Ministry

Acts 16:4-11

They visited many towns, delivering the decision reached
    By the apostles and elders in Jerusalem,
So the churches were strengthened in the faith
    As well as growing daily in numbers.
The Holy Spirit told them not to preach in Asia, so they
    Traveled in Galatia. The Holy Spirit wouldn't let
Them go to the north or south, so they kept going west
    Till they came to the port city of Troas on the Aegean Sea.

That night Paul had a vision of a Macedonian man
    Who said to him, "Come to Macedonia and help us."

Almost immediately they arranged passage to Macedonia
    Convinced God had called them to preach there.

Lord, You guide many ways,
    Thank You for guiding Paul by a vision.
May I always follow Your directions,
    No matter how You speak to me.

Amen

First Mission in Europe

Acts 16:12-40

Luke joined them and they sailed to Philippi, a Roman city
    That was the major city of that district.
After several days they went to the river's edge where women
    Met for prayer on the Sabbath day. There Paul preached to the
        women.

One of them was Lydia, a worshiper of God who
      Had a business selling purple dye. She opened her heart
      To believe all that Paul was saying.
Lydia was baptized along with all her household, and
      She asked Paul and his companions to be her guests, saying,
"If you think I am a true believer, then come
      Stay in my home," and they did.

Lord, thank You that Paul came west with the Gospel
      For it finally came to America and reached me.
May I be as faithful in telling others about Jesus
      As was Paul in his missionary ministry.

As Paul was going to the place of prayer,
      He met a slave girl who predicted the future by demon possession;
      She earned a lot of money for her master this way.
The girl followed Paul and his companions, shouting,
      "These men are servants of the Most High God,
      They tell us how to be saved."
She kept this up until Paul became so irritated that he turned,
      Spoke to the demon, "I command you in the
      Name of Jesus Christ to come out of her."
The demon came out of her immediately, and when her owner
      Saw that his hope of making more money was gone,
Seized Paul and Silas and dragged them before the authorities
      In the market square, where they charged them,
"These men are Jews who are advocating practices which
      Are unlawful for us as Romans to accept or follow."
A crowd quickly formed and began yelling against them,
      So the magistrates had them stripped and flogged.
They were given many lashes, then thrown in prison and
      Told the jailer to keep a close watch on them.
He followed the instructions, threw them into the inner prison,
      And locked their feet in stocks.

That night, Paul and Silas were praying and singing
        Psalms to God while the other prisoners listened.
Suddenly, an earthquake shook the prison; the doors flew open
        And the chains fell off all the prisoners.

Lord, as Paul and Silas fellowshipped with You in prayer,
        And worshiped You with psalms,
        The doors were opened and the chains fell off their hands.
I know this was Your miracle for You came to receive
        Their worship. Jesus said, "You seek worship."
I know You don't need doors to open for Your entrance,
        But it was a nice touch in this situation.

The jailer awakened and saw the doors open, so he drew his sword
        And was about to commit suicide, thinking his prisoners had escaped.
Paul shouted, "Don't harm yourself, we are all here";
        The jailer got a light and rushed in to fall at the feet
        Of Paul and Silas, asking, "What must I do to be saved?"
They replied, "Believe in Jesus Christ and you will be saved,
        You and your household." Then Paul explained
        The Word of the Lord to him and all those in the house.
The jailer washed their wounds, then he and his family
        Were baptized. He brought them into his house
        And fed them a meal.
The whole family celebrated their conversion and
        Belief in God.
When morning came, the magistrates sent a message
        To the jailers to release them.
Paul said, "No! They have beaten us publicly without a trial,
        Despite the fact we are Roman citizens. They can't get rid of us
        quietly;
        Let them come and release us themselves."
The magistrates were frightened when they heard they were Romans,
        So they came to the jail and begged them to leave the city.

Paul and Silas returned to Lydia's home and preached words
  Of encouragement to them before they left the city.

Lord, thank You for providentially protecting Paul's life;
  I know a child of God is immortal and death can't touch them
  Until You have finished Your will for them on earth.

Amen

The New Church at Thessalonica and Berea

Acts 17:1-14

Lord, Paul traveled to Thessalonica and entered the Synagogue
  As was his custom. He debated with the Jews for three weeks
  Explaining and proving the Messiah must suffer and be resurrected.
Paul explained the Messiah is Jesus. Some were convinced and
  Joined Paul and Silas, as well as many God-fearing Gentiles,
  Many of these where rich women.
The unbelieving Jews resented Paul and recruited a gang of thugs
  From the marketplace to riot against Christians in the city.
They ran to Jason's home hoping to find Paul and Silas,
  And bring them before the city officials.
When they didn't find them, they dragged Jason
  And another person to court charging, "These men
  Who have turned the world up side down, have come here now."
"They defy Caesar's decree, saying, 'There is another King called Jesus;'"
  When they heard this, the crowd and city officials were alarmed;
  They made Jason post a bond before releasing them.

Lord, help me be faithful in the face of opposition.
  You've turned my private world upside down.
  May I become a witness to those I meet in life.

The Christians immediately sent Paul and Silas inland to Berea,
>   There Paul went into the Jewish Synagogue and spoke.
The Bereans were more fair-minded than the Thessalonians
>   In that they gave an example how to listen to the Word of God.

Lord, I will receive the word of God with an open mind,
>   *I will search—daily—every part of Scripture*
>   *To determine what You have said for me to believe and live.*

The Jews from Thessalonica heard that Paul was preaching in Berea,
>   So they went there to stir up a riot.
The Christians arranged for Paul to leave immediately,
>   Silas and Timothy were left to build up the church;
>   An escort went with Paul to Athens, the capitol city.

Lord, give me a love and reverence for Your Word.
>   *May I study it carefully—every word—to know what you've said.*
Give me a passion to live a holy productive life for You.
>   *May my life be based on the principles I've learned from Your*
>   *Word.*

Amen

Paul Preaching in Athens

Acts 17:15-34

While waiting for Silas and Timothy, Paul was upset
>   Because the whole city of Athens was worshiping idols.
Paul debated in the Synagogue with the Jews and God-fearing Gentiles
>   As well as in the city market with those gathered there.
While speaking, some Epicurean and stoic philosophers listened to him
>   And they remarked, "What is this babbler trying to say?"
They accused Paul of advocating a foreign God
>   Because he was preaching Jesus and the resurrection.

They brought Paul to the forum at Mars Hill, asking,
      "Tell us more about this religion that you're preaching."
They accused Paul of saying startling things
      And they wanted to find out more about it.
(The Athenians and foreigners who lived there spent their time
      Discussing the latest new ideas),
      So Paul stood to address the whole forum.
"Men of Athens, I see that you are very religious,
      Because as I walked about this place, I saw many idols."
      "I even saw one with the inscription, 'TO AN UNKNOWN GOD,'
      The God I worship, is the One you don't know.
      "This is the God who created the world and everything in it;
      He does not make His home in shrines built by humans,
      Nor does He need anything humans can do for Him
      Because He is the One who gives everything to everyone,
      Including their life and breath."
      "God created one ancestor, the whole human race comes from
          one man
      And they scattered over the whole face of the earth."
      "God has determined the times of their existence
      And the limits where they lived."
      "God wants all to search for Him so they might find Him
      Because God is not far from each one of us,
      For in Him we live and move and exist."

      "Some of your writers have said, 'We are all His children';
      Since we are the children of God, we should not think
      Of deity in terms of gold, silver or a carved statue."
      "God overlooks this sort of mistake when we are ignorant,
      But now He tells everyone everywhere to repent
      Because God has set a date when He will judge the world."
      "God appointed a Man to judge rightly,
      And proved this to us by raising that man from the dead."
When they heard about the resurrection of the dead, some laughed,

Others said, "We would like to hear about this again."
At this time, Paul left the forum, but some joined him
    And became believers, among them Dionysius
    The Acropagite, a woman named Damaris, and some others.

May I have opportunities to tell people what You've done for me.
    I want to tell people the Gospel who've never heard it correctly;
    I want to be used by You, as You used Paul.

Amen

Paul at Corinth

Acts 18:1-17

Lord, Paul left Athens and went to Corinth
    Where he stayed in the home of Aquila, the tent maker.
Aquila with his wife, Priscilla, were originally from Turkey,
    But recently they were thrown out of Rome because
    All Jews were expelled by Claudius the Emperor.
Paul worked for them for he was a tentmaker.
    Every Sabbath Paul debated in the Synagogue
    Trying to convert Jews as well as Gentiles who attended.
After Silas and Timothy came from Macedonia,
    Paul spent his full time testifying to the Jews
    That Jesus was the Messiah.
When the Jews threatened Paul, he shook the dust off of his robe and
    said,
    "Your blood be upon your own hands. From now on
    I will preach the gospel to the Gentiles with a clear conscience."
Paul then moved the church into the house of Justus,
    A believer who lived next to the Synagogue.
Crispus, the leader of the Synagogue, became a believer
    And a great many Corinthians also believed and were baptized.

Therefore the Lord spoke to Paul in a vision at night saying,
　　　"Don't be afraid of leaving the Synagogue to worship in a
　　　house;
Continue speaking because I'll be with you, no one will harm you,
　　　I have many in this city who will become believers."
So Paul stayed in Corinth for eighteen months, preaching the Scriptures.

Lord, thank You for my church that nourishes me.
　　　I'm glad you approved the example of separating
　　　The church from the Jewish Synagogue.

When Gallio became governor of the region, the Jews banned together
　　　To bring Paul before him for trial, accusing him,
"This man persuades people to worship God that break our law";
　　　Before Paul could speak, Gallio said,
"Listen you Jews! If this were a matter of breaking the law,
　　　I would not hesitate to listen to your charges,
But you are bickering about words and your religious laws,
　　　Settle the matter outside the court room;
　　　I do not intend to make a legal decision about religious matters."
Gallio sent them out of the court room, and a crowd
　　　Jumped on Sosthenes, the leader of the Synagogue, and beat him
　　　In front of the court house;
　　　But Gallio paid no attention to it.

Lord, thank You for living in a country that
　　　Has separation of church and state.
I will fully support my state as You command;
　　　I will fully support my church
　　　Which is my Christian duty.

　　　　　　　Amen

Paul's Trip to Jerusalem

Acts 18:18-28

After this, Paul left Corinth and sailed for Syria
    Accompanied by Aquila and Priscilla.
Paul shaved his hair according to Jewish custom
    Because his long hair represented a vow he had made.
When they arrived at Ephesus, Paul went into the Synagogue
    To debate with the Jews about Jesus the Messiah.
They asked Paul to stay a few days, but he declined
    Because of his travel schedule.
However he promised, "I will come back if God allows me to do it";
    Paul left Aquila and Priscilla there before sailing away.
When Paul landed at Caesarea, he went up to Jerusalem
    To greet the saints there, then he returned to Antioch at Syria
    The church that sent him on the missionary trip.
After spending some time in Antioch, Paul began his third
    Missionary trip through Turkey, strengthening
    The churches he had established on the two preceding trips.

Lord, help me be sensitive to the leading of the Holy Spirit
    To follow You obediently, as did Paul.

An Alexandrian Jew named Apollos came to preach in Ephesus;
    He was exceptionally eloquent with a firm grasp of Scripture.
Apollos preached boldly and enthusiastically in the Synagogue
    But he only knew what John the Baptist said about the coming
        Christ.
When Priscilla and Aquila heard Apollos preach, they invited him
    To their home to explain to him
    The way of salvation more fully.
When Apollos left for Turkey, the brethren wrote a
    Letter of introduction to the churches, asking them to receive him.
When Apollos arrived, he strengthened the Christians there,

And vigorously refuted the Jews in public debate,
Proving from Scripture that Jesus was the Messiah.

Lord, thank You for lay people like Aquila and Priscilla
Who know the Scriptures, and teach others.
May I be a faithful teacher like them.

Amen

Paul's Ministry in Ephesus

Acts 19:1-41

Lord, while Apollos continued ministering at Corinth,
Paul traveled through Turkey to arrive at Ephesus
Where he found 12 followers of John the Baptist
Who were still preaching baptism of repentance,
Looking forward to the coming of Messiah.
Paul asked them, "Did you receive the Holy Spirit when you believed?"
They answered "No, we don't know anything about the Holy Spirit."
Then Paul asked, "What did you confess when you were baptized?"
They answered, "Belief in the Messiah who is coming."
When Paul pointed out Jesus the Messiah had come,
They were baptized immediately in the name of Jesus.
When Paul laid his hands on them,
The Holy Spirit came on them, and they spoke in tongues.

Lord, I thank You for zealous people like these 12 men
Who are willing to go anywhere to serve You,
Even when they don't have the full truth.
Because you have given me spiritual insight and I know the truth,
May I always be willing to serve You that zealously.

Lord, Paul spoke for three months in the Synagogue,
Debating about Jesus and the Kingdom of God.

When the attitude of the congregation hardened
>   And they began attacking the Way publicly,
>   Paul took believers out of the Synagogue.
They met daily in the school of Tyrannus,
>   Where believers were instructed in the Word of God
>   And the gospel was spread throughout the region.

Lord, I thank You for the church where I heard the Word,
>   *And thank You for the church that spreads the gospel.*

Lord, Paul's ministry included healing the sick through prayer;
>   His handkerchiefs were taken to the sick
>   And they were healed because of their faith.
Some itinerant Jewish evangelist who cast out demons came to Ephesus
>   And spoke the name of "Jesus as preached by Paul."
The man Sceva, a Jewish chief priest, and his seven sons,
>   Tried to cast out a demon who answered,
>   "Jesus I know, and Paul I know; but who are you?"
The demon-possessed man attacked them and beat them mercilessly,
>   He ripped their clothes off them,
>   So that they ran out of the house, naked.
When people in Ephesus heard about the episode,
>   Both Jews and Gentiles were impressed, and they were
>   Afraid to attack Christianity; so the gospel spread everywhere.
Many new believers came forward to repent of their evil deeds;
>   Those who practiced magic and sorcery
>   Burned their incantation books and charms in a big public fire.
Someone estimated their value at 10,000 pieces of silver;
>   As a result the Word of God became more influential
>   And its message was spread widely.

Lord, I will always be willing to rid my life of anything
>   *That is used by satan to deceive and destroy people.*

After this happened, Paul decided to visit Greece
      On his way to Rome, so he sent
      Timothy and Erastus to prepare the way.
About this time a riot broke out against Christianity in Ephesus;
      It began when Demetrius a silversmith called together
      Many of the craftsmen who made silver idols of Diana.
He said, "Paul has persuaded many that our idols are not gods,
      And our sales are going down. Not only here but in all Turkey,
      Paul is destroying the idol trade market."
"Paul is also desecrating our Temple dedicated to Diana
      And reducing worship of Diana over the whole world."
They began to chant, "Great is Diana of the Ephesians"
      And the whole town rushed into the amphitheater
      Dragging along the believers, Gaius and Aristarchus.
Paul wanted to go make an appeal to the crowd,
      But for safety sake the Christians wouldn't let him enter;
      Roman officers also sent messages telling Paul not to go there.
The crowd was confused, some shouting one thing, others another;
      Most didn't even know about the "silversmith" controversy.
A Jew named Alexander was pushed to the front
      But the crowd wouldn't let him speak;
      They shouted, for two hours, "Great is Diana of the Ephesians."
The town clerk eventually quieted the crowd and told them,
      "Everyone knows the greatness of Diana who guards our Temple,
      We all know she fell from Heaven."
"If Demetrius and the craftsmen want to complain,
      Let them take their case to court."
"We must raise our questions in a regular city council,
      Otherwise, Rome will charge us with rioting
      And send soldiers to investigate or punish us."
The clerk then dismissed the crowd and they left.

Lord, help me see Your plan for my life when there is civic turmoil,
      May I always trust You to protect me in strife.

Amen

Paul's Last Trip to Ephesus

Acts 20:1-38

Lord, thank You for protecting Paul's life and giving him wisdom
When to be bold, and in this case, to avoid confrontation.

After Paul encouraged the Christians in Ephesus, he said goodbye,
And set sail for Greece. He stayed there three months.
As Paul was planning to leave by ship, he discovered a
Plot to kill him by the Jews. So he went by land
Through northern Greece.
Paul had many traveling with him for protection; Sopater,
Aristarchus, Secundus, Gaius, Timothy, Tychicus,
And Trophimus.
After celebrating the Passover, Paul left Philippi and
Boarded a ship for Troas in Turkey.
On Sunday, Paul observed the Lord's Table, then preached
A long sermon that went on into the night.
The room was hot because a large number of lamps were burning;
Eutychus, a young man sitting on the window sill,
Fell asleep and then fell three stories to the ground.
He was picked up dead, but Paul went down and embraced him
Saying, "Don't worry, there is life in him."
Paul went back upstairs where he ate a meal, then
He talked until daybreak and then left.
They took the boy home alive, and all praised God.

Lord, thank You for healing the young man;
Now I know You will take care of me physically.

Paul visited several cities as he traveled toward Jerusalem;
He decided not to visit Ephesus, but had the elders

Come meet him at the ship in Miletus.
Paul told them, "You know how honestly I lived since I came here,
How I served the Lord in all humility,
How I remained faithful, even when the Jews plotted against me."
"I never hesitated to tell you the truth,
Both publicly and in your homes."
"I have declared to both Jews and Gentiles
That they must repent and put their faith in our Lord Jesus."
"Now you know the Holy Spirit is leading me to Jerusalem,
But I don't know what will happen to me there;
Except that the Holy Spirit in city after city has let me know
That persecution and imprisonment await me in Rome."
"But my life will be spent finishing the race
That I have been running in the mission the Lord Jesus gave me,
And that is spreading the Good News of God's grace."
"Now I feel sure that none of you will see me again;
My conscience is clear concerning my work among you
For I have declared the whole Gospel among you."
"Guard yourselves and the flock that the Holy Spirit has given you;
Be a good example in leading them in godliness
And feed the church which is bought with Christ's blood."
"I know when I have gone, false teachers will come
Who will not have compassion on the flock."
"Also, men from among yourselves will distort the truth
To draw away disciples to follow them."
"So be on your guard, remember that night and day
I kept constant watchcare over the flock,
Shedding many tears for you in prayer."
"Now I commit you to God and the word of His grace
Which will give you an inheritance among the saints."
"I never asked anyone for money or clothes;
You know I worked to earn money to meet my needs."
"I did this to be a constant example to the church

To help the poor, for I remember the words of Jesus,
'It is more blessed to give than to receive.'"
When Paul finished speaking, they knelt on the beach and prayed;
Then they wept and embraced Paul because
He said they wouldn't see him again.

Lord, thank You for friends who pray for me
As the elders prayed for the apostle Paul.
Raise up my prayer supporters who will intercede
For me as I live and serve You.

Amen

Paul Goes to Jerusalem

Acts 21:1-40

Lord, I see how You protected Paul in many small ways,
Do the same for me, protecting me through the hum-drum of life.

Paul sailed from Troas to Lebanon, stopping at several places,
The ship landed at Tyre, there Paul stayed a week;
The Christians kept telling Paul not to go to Jerusalem.
Paul then sailed to Caesarea, and stayed with Phillip the evangelist
Who had four daughters in ministry;
He was one of the original seven deacons.
After several days, Agabus the prophet arrived to see Paul;
He took the belt on Paul's tunic and tied his hands and feet
Saying, "The owner of this belt will be bound hand and foot in
Jerusalem and then be handed over to the Gentiles."
Everyone who heard this begged Paul not to go to Jerusalem
But he replied, "Why are you crying to change my mind?"
"I am ready not only to be bound in Jerusalem, but to die
For the name of the Lord Jesus."

When the crowd saw they couldn't change Paul's mind, they said,
    "The will of the Lord be done.

Lord, give me resolute determination to follow You,
    Even when it seems dangerous and life threatening.

Paul left to go up to Jerusalem, Christians from Caesarea
    Went with him to the home of Mnason from Cyprus
    Who had been one of the earliest disciples.
The brothers gave Paul a warm welcome when Paul arrived in Jerusalem:
    The next day Paul visited James and the elders.
Then Paul gave them a detailed account of what God had done
    Among the Gentiles through his ministry;
    The brothers gave glory to God when they heard it.
Then the elders told Paul, "There are thousands of Jews
    Who have been saved, who staunchly uphold the law."
"They have heard that you tell Jewish Christians to break with Moses,
    And you authorize them not to circumcise their children."
"They will certainly hear that you are here and
    Will want a meeting with you."
"Here is what we suggest you do. We have four men who
    Have taken a Nazarite vow. You go with them
    To the Temple to be purified with them."
"You pay the Temple expenses connected with shaving their heads;
    This will let everyone know you keep the Law
    And that there is no truth in the rumors about you."
"As for Gentile believers, we aren't asking them to observe
    These Temple customs. The only thing they must do is,
Not eat food offered to idols, and not eat unbled meat
    From animals that are strangled, and avoid fornication."
The next day Paul went with the four men to the ceremony
    To be purified, and announced that in seven days
    They would offer sacrifices to end the vow.
When the seven days were almost over, some Jews from Asia,

Saw Paul in the Temple and began a riot, shouting,

"Men of Israel! This man preaches to everyone, everywhere

That it is wrong to keep the Law and worship in the Temple."

"He has profaned the Holy Place by bringing Gentiles here."

But they were wrong; they had seen Trophimus from Ephesus

With Paul in the city and thought he brought him into the Temple.

People came running from every direction, they grabbed Paul

And dragged him out of the Temple;

The gates were closed behind them.

The crowd would have killed Paul, but Roman soldiers intervened

Because their officer heard there was rioting in the city.

The soldiers stopped the crowd from beating Paul;

The Roman officer arrested Paul and chained his hands and feet;

Then he asked Paul to identify himself.

The crowd called out different things and made it impossible

For the officer to get a positive identification of Paul.

Paul was carried by the soldiers to the stairs because

The crowd was so violent. They were shouting, "Kill him."

When Paul spoke to the officer, he was surprised Paul spoke Greek;

Then the officer said, "You're not the Egyptian who led

An insurrection of 4,000 cut throats."

Lord, thank You for physical protection of Paul

In the middle of chaos and hostility.

Protect me as You did Paul when danger comes;

I will trust You in all things.

Amen

Paul Speaks to a Crowd in Jerusalem

Acts 22:1-30

Paul answered, "I am a Jew, a citizen of Tarsus in Turkey;
    Give me permission to speak to the people."
Paul stood at the top of the stairs and gestured to the crowd,
    And when they became quiet, he spoke in Hebrew,
"My brothers, and fathers, listen to my defense;"
    When the crowd heard him speaking in Hebrew,
    They became still, even more quiet than before.
"I am a Jew, and was born in Tarsus of Turkey. In this city
    I studied under Gamaliel and was taught to obey
    Every Jewish law and custom."
    "In fact, I was so devoted—as you are today—I even
    Persecuted Christians, binding them to death,
    Delivering both men and women in chains to prison."
    "The High priest or any member of the Sanhedrin
    Will testify to these facts."
    "I ask a letter from them to their brothers in Damascus
    To do the same there. I set off to go to Damascus
    To bring back prisoners to Jerusalem for punishment."
    "I was nearly to Damascus when at noon a bright light
    From Heaven blinded me. I fell to the ground and heard a voice,
    'Saul, Saul, why are you persecuting Me?' I answered,
    "Who are You, Lord?" He answered,
    'I am Jesus of Nazareth, whom you are persecuting.'"
    "The people with me saw the light, but didn't understand the voice,"
I said, 'What do you want me to do?' The Lord answered,
    "Stand up, go to Damascus, it will be told you what to do."
    "The light was so blinding my companions
    Had to lead me to Damascus by the hand."

Lord, I cannot deny the experiences of life.
    Thank You for those who brought the Gospel to me,
    Thank You for events that led to my conversion.

"A man named Ananias, a devout follower of the Law,
    And highly respected by the Jewish community,
    Came to pray beside me and said, 'Brother Saul, receive your sight.'"
"Then he said, 'God has chosen you
    To do His will, to see the Messiah, and to carry out His message;
    You will be a witness to all people what you have seen and heard.'
    'Why delay? It's time to be baptized as a sign your
    Sins are forgiven.'
    "When I got back to Jerusalem, I was praying in the Temple,
    In a trance, I saw the Lord who said, 'Hurry
    Leave Jerusalem, they will not receive your testimony.'"
    "Lord," I prayed, "is it because I arrested and beat those who
    Believed in You?"
    "When Stephen's blood was being shed, I gave consent
    And watched the coats of those who stoned him."
    "Then the Lord said to me, 'Go, I will send you to the Gentiles'";
The crowd listened to Paul until he said the word *Gentiles*,
    Then they shouted, 'Away with him, he is not fit to live.'"
The Jews yelled, threw dust into the air, and waved their coats;
    So the commanding officer took Paul into the fortress.

Lord, thank You for Paul's witness in the face of opposition;
    Give me boldness to testify for You when danger comes.

He ordered Paul to be examined under the whip to find out the truth;
    When they strapped Paul down, he said to the Centurion,
    "Is it legal for you to scourge an uncondemned Roman citizen?"
The Centurion told his superior, "This man is a Roman citizen;"
    The commander asked if Paul were a Roman citizen;
    "I am," was Paul's reply.

The commander replied, "It cost me a large amount of money to become
A citizen." Paul replied, "I was free born";
The soldiers who were going to flog Paul quickly left.
The commander was frightened because he could have been punished
For scourging a Roman citizen.
The next day the commander took off Paul's chains;
He ordered the Sanhedrin to meet with the Chief Priest,
Then brought Paul to stand before them.

Lord, Paul used a legal means to escape punishment;
Give me wisdom not to be punished needlessly
And give me courage to accept punishment when need be.

Amen

Paul Before the Jewish Council

Acts 23:1-35

Lord, Paul looked intently at the Sanhedrin, then spoke,
"My brothers, I have always lived with a perfectly clear conscience."
Immediately, Ananias the High Priest ordered those near Paul
To slap him on the mouth. Paul responded, "God strike you,
You filthy wall that's been whitewashed."
Paul asked, "How can you break the Law striking me
Before I am found guilty?"
The men close to Paul said, "You're insulting God's High Priest;"
Paul answered, "I did not realize it was the High Priest,
Because Scripture says, 'Don't curse the ruler of the people.'"
Paul became aware that the Sanhedrin was split between
The Sadducees and the Pharisees, so he called out,
"I am on trial for the hope of the resurrection."
Instantly, a debate broke out between the two opposing factions

And the assembly was evenly split.
The Sadducees don't believe in the resurrection, angels, or eternal spirits,
       but Pharisees believe all these.
They shouted loudly at each other, and the Pharisees said,
       "We find nothing wrong with this man;
       Perhaps a spirit or angel spoke to him at his conversion."
The Roman commander fearing they would physically beat Paul,
       Ordered his troops to enter and take Paul to the fortress.
That night the Lord stood by Paul saying, "Be courageous,
       You have witnessed for Me in Jerusalem
       Now you must witness for Me in Rome."

Lord, help me to be more courageous as was Paul
       Even when I find myself in peaceful surroundings.

Early in the morning, about 40 Jews held a secret meeting
       And vowed an oath not to eat until they killed Paul.
They told the Chief Priest and elders, "We have vowed to fast
       Until we kill Paul, now it is your responsibility to ask
       The commander to return Paul so you can examine him closely."
"It is our responsibility to kill him in the streets
       As they bring him to you."
The son of Paul's sister heard their plans of ambush
       And came to the fortress to tell Paul;
       He immediately had the boy taken to the commander.
When the boy was brought to the commander, they went privately
       Where the boy said, "There are 40 Jews who have vowed
       Not to eat until they have killed Paul."
"These Jews will get the Sanhedrin to request you to bring Paul
       To be questioned more closely, they plan to kill him in the streets;
       They are waiting your order to deliver Paul."
The commander let the boy go, warning him, "Don't tell anyone
       You've given me this information."
The commander commanded two of his centurions, "Get 200

Soldiers ready immediately. Leave now in the dark with

200 spearmen and 70 mounted cavalry. Put Paul on a horse,

Get him safely to Caesarea and Governor Felix."

The commander wrote a letter,

This man was seized by the Jews and they were

Attempting to kill him, so I commanded my troops

To arrest him. Then I discovered he was a Roman citizen.

I took him to their Sanhedrin to find out what charge

Could be brought against him. I discovered it was about

Their Jewish doctrine, nothing worthy of imprisonment.

When I was informed of a plot to assassinate him,

I decided to send him to you and tell his accusers

To bring their charge before you.

The soldiers carried out their orders and took Paul down from

Jerusalem to the Mediterranean Sea. Then the mounted soldiers

Took Paul the rest of the way to Caesarea, and then returned.

When Felix got the letter, he asked Paul where he was born,

Then hearing it was Turkey said, "I will hear your case,

As soon as your accusers come from Jerusalem."

Then Felix ordered Paul held in prison in Herod's Palace.

Lord , I marvel at the way You work in small details,

You allowed the nephew to warn the Roman Commander.

Lord, I thank You that the total might of the Roman Empire was used

To protect Your servant so he could preach the Gospel in Rome.

Thank You for working in little and big ways.

Amen

Paul Before Felix

Acts 24:1-27

Lord, I see Your hand working through politics and big government.
        After five days, the High Priest, Ananias, some elders,
        And the lawyer named Tertullus appeared in court in Caesarea.
When Tertullus was called, he brought their case before Felix,
        "Your Excellency, you have given peace and protection
        To the Jews and changed bad laws that persecuted us.
        "At all times, and in all places, we acknowledge
        What you've done for all Jews—with our gratitude."
        "I don't want to take up too much of your time,
        So let me tell you briefly what this man—Paul—has done."
        "He is a trouble-maker, stirring up trouble among the Jews
        Worldwide, and is the ring leader of the sect of the Nazarenes."
        "He attempted to profane the Temple. We placed him
        Under arrest by the Temple guards and planned to judge
        Him by our laws, but the Roman Commander Lysias intervened
        And used force to take him out of our hands, then ordered
        Him to appear before you. Ask him, he will tell you the truth."
The Jews who came with their lawyer agreed to the charges,
        So Felix motioned Paul to speak.
Paul answered, "I know you have been a fair judge over the Jews
        For many years. Therefore, I defend myself with confidence."
        "Only 12 days ago I made my pilgrimage to Jerusalem,
        I was not arguing with anyone in the Temple
        Or their synagogues throughout town, neither can they
        Prove their accusations they made against me."

        "I will admit that I worship the God of my ancestors,
        According to the Way which they call a sect."
        "I firmly believe in Jewish law and everything written in the
        Prophets. I believe, just as my accusers, that there

Will be a resurrection of the righteous and wicked. I strive
To keep my conscience clear before God and man."

"After several years of absence, I came bringing alms for the
Poor and to present offerings to God; it was in this connection
That the Jews found me in the Temple. I was purified
And there was no crowd with me and no disturbance."
"Some Jews from Turkey saw me there—these are the ones
Who should testify against me—because they said I desecrated
The Temple by bringing in Gentiles; but the Gentiles were not
with me." "Therefore, I am not guilty of causing a riot.
If anything, these Jews caused the riot."

"I am guilty of one thing. When I was brought before the
Sanhedrin, I called out about the resurrection which caused a
Great argument."

Felix, who knew more about the Way than most people,
    Adjourned the proceedings saying, "When Lysias
    Comes, I will decide this case."
Felix ordered the Roman commander to keep Paul under guard,
    But gave him some freedom and allowed his friends to come to him.
A few days later, Felix and his wife Drusilla, who was Jewish,
    Sent for Paul for a hearing on the subject of faith in Christ.
As Paul spoke about righteousness and self-discipline
    And judgment to come, Felix was terrified, saying,
"You may go for now. When I have a more convenient time,
    I'll call for you." He hoped Paul would pay him money
    So Felix frequently summoned Paul to talk with him.
Felix wanted to gain favor with the Jews, so he left Paul in prison;
    Two years went by and Felix was replaced by Festus.

Lord, thank You for Paul's positive witness before government officials;
    May I always give a clear witness to Your faithfulness.

Amen

Paul Before Festus

Acts 25:1-27

Lord, I understand government officials represent Your power,
Thank You for Your law that gives me security in my culture.

When Festus took up his appointment, he visited Jerusalem
Where the Chief Priest and Jewish leaders asked him
To do something immediately about the case of Paul.
They wanted Festus to side with them and asked for Paul
To be transferred back to Jerusalem, because they planned
To ambush and murder him on the highway.
Festus told them Paul would remain in custody in Caesarea
And that he would hold court there shortly.
Festus said, "Send your authorities to Caesarea with me,
And if Paul is guilty, you can bring charges against him."
Festus stayed in Jerusalem for about 10 days, then returned to Caesarea;
The next day he had Paul brought before the tribunal.
Almost immediately the Jews surrounded Paul and brought
Accusations against him, but didn't have any proof.
Paul defended himself, "I have committed no offense against
The Temple or against Caesar."
Festus was anxious to please the Jews, so he asked Paul,
"Are you willing to go to Jerusalem to stand trial?"
But Paul answered, "No! I am standing before the tribunal of Caesar,
Where I should be tried. I demand my hearing
Before Caesar himself. I have done the Jews no wrong,
As you very well know. I am not guilty of any civil
Crime. I do not ask to be spared from death, but
Since there is no substance to their charges, no one has
The right to surrender me to them. I appeal to Caesar."
Then Festus conferred with his legal advisors and concluded,
"You have appealed to Caesar, to Caesar you should go."

Lord, I thank You that the government protected Paul from death,
    Thank You for the protection I have by my government.

A few days later, King Agrippa and Bernice arrived in Caesarea
    To pay a visit to Festus. They stayed several days.
Festus explained Paul's case to them,
    "I have a man in prison that Felix left there."
    "While I was in Jerusalem, the Chief Priest and the leader of the
        Jews
    Demanded his condemnation. I told them Roman law does
    Not surrender a prisoner, until the accused has an opportunity
    To confront his accusers and is given an opportunity to
    Defend himself. So they came here to Caesarea and I
    Took the tribunal seat and brought the man before me."
    "The accusers did not charge him with any crime."
    "They argued religious doctrine and about a dead man called Jesus
    Whom Paul alleged to be alive. Not feeling qualified to deal with
    This question, I asked if he would be willing to go to Jerusalem
    To be tried on this issue. Paul appealed his case
    To the judgment seat of Caesar, so I have held him
    Until I could send him to Rome."
Agrippa said, "I would like to hear the man myself." Festus
    Answered, "Tomorrow you shall hear him."
The next day Agrippa and Bernice arrived in great ceremony
    Entering the court room with the officials of the city;
    Then Festus ordered Paul to be brought in.
Festus said, "King Agrippa and all who are present today,
    See this man. The whole Jewish community has
    Petitioned me that he should not live. For my part,
    I'm satisfied he hasn't committed a capital crime."
    "But he appealed to Caesar, so I decided to send him there."
    "Since I have no definite crime that I can write to Caesar,
    I am presenting him here before you,
    King Agrippa, and all these officials so that after you examine him,

I will have an accusation against him."
"It seems pointless to send a prisoner to Caesar without
Charges against him."

Paul Before King Agrippa

Acts 26:1-32

Lord, I'll be grateful for opportunities to witness in official places for You;
  If I'm ever given the opportunity,
  May I do it with power.

King Agrippa said to Paul, "You may speak in Your defense";
  Paul gestured for silence, then spoke,
  "I am fortunate to be able to defend myself before you, King
      Agrippa,
  Because I know you are an expert on Jewish customs and law."
  "So please listen to my whole defense."
  "Everyone knows I was trained from my childhood in Jewish
  Tradition and completed my education in Jerusalem."
  "The Jews have known that I lived in the strictest way among them
  As a Pharisee. But the reason the Jews have charged me is
  Something else. It is for the promise made to the fathers."
  "It is the promise of the resurrection from the dead and eternal life,
  This is why I have been put on trial by the Jews."
  "Does it seem incredible that God can raise the dead?"

  "I did all I could to oppose the name of Jesus of Nazareth,
  That is how I spent my time in Jerusalem. I put many
  Saints into prison on the authority of the Chief Priest."
  "When they voted to stone Stephen, I voted with them."
  "Many times I visited synagogues to punish Christians

Trying to force them to renounce their faith. I was
So angry against Christians that I pursued them to foreign cities."

"I was on one of these journeys to Damascus with authority
From the Chief Priest. About mid-day on the road
I saw a light—brighter than the sun—from Heaven."
"It shone brilliantly around me and my fellow travelers, so that
We fell to the ground. I heard a voice saying to me
In Hebrew, 'Saul, Saul, why are you persecuting me?
Your kicking is only hurting yourself.'"
"Then I answered, 'Who are you Lord?'"
"The Lord answered me, 'I am Jesus whom you are persecuting.
Get up and stand on your feet, for I have a reason
For appearing to you—to appoint you to be my servant,
And be a witness to tell everyone you have seen Me,
I will protect you from your people."
"I will send you to the Gentiles, to open their eyes
To their blinded condition, so they may turn from darkness
To light, from satan's control to God's service; so their
Sins can be forgiven, and they can receive the inheritance
Of eternal life."
"After that, King Agrippa, I was not disobedient to the
Heavenly vision. I began immediately preaching to the people
Of Damascus, then to those in Jerusalem, and all the countryside
Of Judea, and also to Gentiles; urging them to repent
And turn to God; then prove their repentance by doing good works."

"The Jews arrested me in the Temple for doing this, and
Tried to kill me, but God has protected me to this very hour."

"Therefore, I stand before you to testify to both high officials
And the lowest of people alike; the same thing the prophets
And Moses said would happen; that Christ would first suffer,
And then rise from the dead to proclaim the light of salvation
To the Jews and also to the Gentiles."

Festus jumped to his feet and shouted, "Paul you're mad, your learning
    Has made you insane."

Paul answered, "Festus, Your Excellency, I am not mad, I
    Am speaking the truth." Then Paul turned to King Agrippa,
    "The King understands these matters. I appeal to him in these
    Matters, knowing he understands these issues, because none
    Of these things were done in secret."
    "King Agrippa, do you believe the things the prophets said?"
    "I know you do!"
Then King Agrippa replied, "Almost you convinced me to become
    A Christian."
Then Paul replied, "I wish you were a Christian, both you and
    Everyone who hears these words. I wish you were the
    Same as I—except these chains."
At this point in Paul's speech, the king arose and with the governor
    And Bernice and other government officials left the room;
    They talked among themselves, saying,
"This man has done nothing that deserves death or imprisonment."
    Agrippa said to Festus, "You should release this man,
    Except he appealed to Caesar."

Lord, thank You for the boldness of Paul's testimony,
    If he had not been faithful, I might not be saved;
    Help me be as faithful as Paul.

Amen

Paul's Trip to Rome

Acts 27:1-44

They finally made arrangements to sail for Italy,
    So they handed Paul and other prisoners over to a Centurion
    Named Julius, of the Augustine regiment.

They boarded a ship that was scheduled to make several stops
    Along the coast of Turkey.
When they reached Lebanon, Julius let Paul go ashore to visit
    Christians and receive hospitality from them.
From there, they put out to sea, but because of stormy winds,
    Sailed north of Cyprus near the coast of Turkey;
    At Myra, they changed ships for one heading to Rome.
The winds were still strong so they sailed under Crete;
    They struggled in the wind until they came to Fair Havens,
    Near the town of Lasea, near Rhodes.
They stayed there several days, because sailing was hazardous
    Because it was winter. So Paul warned the commander,
"Friends, this is going to be a dangerous voyage and there is a risk
    That we will lose the cargo, the ship, and also our lives."
    But the Centurion listened more to the captain and owner than
    to Paul.
Since Fair Havens was an exposed harbor that was a dangerous place
    To spend the winter, they decided to go further;
    Then they decided to winter in Phoenix because it was a
    protected harbor.
Just then a light wind blew from the south that was perfect for sailing;
    They took in the anchor and sailed past Crete, but before long
    A hurricane caught them in open waters.
It was impossible to keep the ship headed into the wind,
    So they gave up and let it run with the wind;
    It was a continual struggle to keep the boat under control.
They hoisted the small life boat being towed behind them,
    Then wrapped ropes around the hull to strengthen it,
    So they dropped a sea anchor and let the ship drift.
The next day when the waves grew higher, they threw
    Cargo overboard. The following day they threw out
    The tackle and ship's gear.
They couldn't see the sun or moon for several days,

So everyone gave up hope of surviving.
When they hadn't eaten for several days, Paul addressed everyone,
 "If you had listened to me, we wouldn't have this damage."
 "Now I ask you don't give up hope. No one will die,
 Only the ship will be lost. Last night God, to whom
 I belong and whom I serve; He sent an angel to tell me
 'Fear not Paul, you will appear before Caesar, therefore all
 Who are sailing with you will be safe.' So be courageous,
 It will happen just as God told me. We will be stranded
 On some island."
On the 14th night the ship was still drifting
 When the sailors felt land was near. They sounded
 And found it was 120 feet of water.
A little later they sounded again and found 90 feet of water;
 They realized they would be driven into rocks, so they
 Threw out four anchors, and prayed for daylight.
Then the sailors planned to abandon the ship, so they lowered
 An emergency boat as though they were putting out anchors.
Paul said to the Centurion, "We will all die unless the sailors
 Stay aboard." The soldiers cut the rope to let the small boat drift
 away.
As it began to get light, Paul urged everyone to eat something
 So they would have strength for the coming emergency.
Paul said, "There's no safety in fasting, not one of you
 Will lose a hair of your head."
Then Paul took bread, gave thanks, broke it, and began to eat;
 Everyone was encouraged and they ate.
There were a total of 276 on board, so then they
 Threw the grain into the sea.
When daybreak gave some light, no one recognized the island,
 But they saw a bay with a beach. They planned
 To run the ship aground on the beach if possible.
They cut the anchors, lowered the rudders, hoisted the top sail,

And headed ashore, but the ship hit a sand bar.
The bow of the boat stuck in the sand and the pounding waves began to
    Break up the stern.
The soldiers planned to kill the prisoners because they were afraid
        They would escape. But the Centurion was determined to
        Deliver Paul safely to Rome. He wouldn't let them do it.
He gave orders for those who could swim to swim to shore,
        He then directed the others to follow on planks or pieces of
        wreckage;
        All escaped safely to the beach.

Lord, You allow your children to be tested in the storms of life,
        Help me be courageous when I'm tested,
        Help me get through storms as did Paul.

Amen

From Malta to Rome

Acts 28:1-31

Lord, when I get through the storms of life,
        I know You'll soothe and comfort me from my pain;
        But help me remember to praise You for deliverance.

When they got on the beach, they discovered it was
        The island of Malta. The inhabitants welcomed them and
        Built a huge fire to warm them.
Paul had collected a bundle of sticks, and as he
        Placed them in the fire, a viper bit him in the hand.
When the inhabitants saw the snake hanging onto Paul's hand,
        They waited for him to die, saying, "He's a
        Terrible sinner, the storm didn't kill him but the snake will."
Paul shook the snake into the fire, but his hand didn't swell up,
        Nor did he drop dead. They changed their minds and said,

"Paul's a god."
They were near an estate belonging to Publius, the governor of the island;
>He fed the survivors for three days.
Publuis' father was in bed suffering from high fever and dysentery,
>Paul laid his hand on him and prayed for him and the man was
>healed;
>When this happened, other sick came and were cured as well.
After three months the winter was over; Paul was ready to leave.
>He set sail for Italy, and the people of the island
>Put provisions on board for Paul and his companions.

When the believers in Rome heard about Paul's arrival,
>They came to meet Paul
>at the Forum of Appius and the Three Taverns;
>Paul thanked God and was encouraged when he saw them.
When Paul arrived in Rome, he was allowed to stay
>In his own rented apartment where soldiers guarded him.

After three days, Paul called the leading Jews for a day's discussion;
>Paul said, "Brothers, although I have done nothing against
>Our people or our customs, I was arrested in Jerusalem,
>And delivered over to the Romans."
"They examined me and would have set me free because they found
>I was not guilty of any crime. But the Jews
>Filed an objection, and I was forced to appeal to Caesar."
"That is why I asked to see you and talk to you about this matter.
>It is for the hope of Israel that I wear these chains."
The Jews answered, "We haven't heard anything against you,
>We haven't received a letter from Jerusalem, nor have
>Any who have arrived here from Judea said anything about you."
"But we want to hear what you believe. All we know
>About Christians is that they are hated everywhere."

Lord, help me have a positive attitude in life
>*Even when I know there are many with negative thoughts about You."*

They set a time so that a large number of Jews
>   Could visit Paul at his apartment to discuss Christianity.
Paul told them that Jesus came to sit on the throne of David,
>   And he argued from the Law of Moses and the Prophet,
>   Trying to persuade them about Jesus.
They began early in the morning and continued until the evening;
>   Some were convinced, but others were skeptical;
>   So the Jews disagreed among themselves.
Paul had one last thing to say to the Jews,
>   "You Jews will hear the Gospel, but not understand,
>   You will see the truth of Jesus, but are spiritually blinded,
>   For your heart is hardened,
>   And your spiritual ears are shut up,
>   And your spiritual eyes are blinded,
>   Because you refuse to believe what is presented
>   Lest your heart receive the Gospel
>   And you become converted and are healed."
Paul understood from that experience that salvation
>   Was to be sent to the Gentiles, because they will listen to God.

Paul spent two years in this rented apartment
>   Welcoming all who came to see him,
Proclaiming the Kingdom of God to all,
>   Teaching the truth about the Lord Jesus Christ
>   With complete freedom and no hindrance.

Lord, thank You for the great influential life of the apostle Paul;
>   *I cannot do all Paul could do,*
>   *So help me to do all that I can do.*
You don't ask that I do the great accomplishments of others
>   *You only ask me to be faithful to my gifts*
>   *And obey your commands. I'll do that.*

Amen

Hebrews

PRAYING THE BOOK OF HEBREWS
1:1–13:25

THE STORY OF WRITING
THE BOOK OF HEBREWS

It was late at night and the candle on the small table reflected the faces of two aged travelers who followed Jesus Christ. Paul, closest to the light, was telling his physician friend, Luke, some of the problems in Jerusalem, "Christians in Jerusalem are going back into the Temple to make blood sacrifices, this is wrong; Jesus is the final sacrifice for sin! Jesus is the Lamb of God Who took away the sins of the world, how can they sacrifice the blood of an animal to forgive their sins?"

Paul explained it may be acceptable for some Christians to go back into the Temple to pray, these didn't like the simplicity of worshiping Jesus in a house church, they wanted the elegance of the Temple. They liked the pomp and ceremony of observing holy days, the Jewish feasts and the Levitical choirs.

Paul reasoned to his friend Luke that the Christians in Jerusalem were comprising by returning to the Temple worship. Gone were the early days when Christians witnessed from house to house. Gone were the early days when they prayed all night for the power of God. Gone were the early days when the leaders of the Sanhedrin persecuted Christians for the miracles done in the name of Jesus Christ.

Luke said to Paul, "Why don't you write a letter to the church in Jerusalem warning them about going back to Temple worship?"

Paul thought about it for a moment and then shook his head, "No!" he explained, "The church in Jerusalem will have nothing to do with me because I am the apostle to the Gentiles." Then Paul added, "The Jewish Christians in Jerusalem would not listen to me, they are so bound up in their traditions that they hate me!"

Then Paul concluded, "Jewish Christians in Jerusalem still will have nothing to do with Gentiles."

Paul thought again about writing a letter to them for a few minutes, then summarized, "No…the church in Jerusalem would not listen to a letter from Paul."

Luke agreed with Paul but he knew something had to be done. Then Luke remembered a sermon that he had heard many times preached by Paul. It was a sermon on the theme *Better*. Luke said, "Your sermon that Christ is *Better* should be written out and sent to the church at Jerusalem."

Because Luke had heard Paul preach the sermon so many times, he began to repeat the sermon to Paul. He had almost memorized it *word for word*. Luke said, "Christ is better than angels…Christ is better than Moses…Christ is better than the high priest…Christ is better than Melchizedek…Christ is better than the sacrifices…Christ is better than the Old Testament tabernacle…Christ is better than the priest who enters into the holy of holies."

Paul laughed! He hadn't realized Luke paid that close attention to his sermon. But when Paul heard Luke repeat his sermon—word for word—an idea crossed Paul's mind. Then the wise apostle said,

"Luke, you write the sermon in your words and in your style, then the Christians in Jerusalem won't know that I have written it. That way, they won't reject the message."

Paul went on to explain that even though the sermon was his idea, it was not important for him to get the credit for writing the letter. Paul wanted the Christians in Jerusalem to get the message that Christ is *Better* than anything the Old Testament had to offer.

Then Luke suggested, "Don't forget about the warnings in your sermon. Several times in the sermon you warn the people what will happen if they go back to their Temple sacrifices."

"Yes," Paul agreed, "add the warnings."

"But one more thing," Paul added. "Don't put your name on the letter—you're a Gentile. The Jerusalem church will reject the letter if it has your name on it."

"That's good," Luke thought.

"I'll begin tonight," Luke replied.

After getting paper and quill, Luke sat at the table and dipped his quill into the black olive oil ink and began to write, "God, who at various times and in various ways spoke in time past to the fathers by the prophets, has in these last days spoken to us by *His* Son...."

Who wrote Hebrews? As a matter of fact, Paul and Luke did such a good job hiding their contribution to the letter, no one in the early church knew for sure who wrote the letter. Some thought Paul, a few thought Luke, some thought Apollos, and a few thought Barnabas. Two hundred years after its writing, Tertullian the Church Father said, "Only God knows for sure who wrote Hebrews."[1]

Endnote

1. See Bible.org, <http://www.bible.org/page.asp?page_id=1360,> (accessed 18 August 2006).

Praying the Book of Hebrews

Jesus Is Better Than the Prophets

Hebrews 1:1-3

Lord, long ago You spoke in many different ways at many different times
> To past believers, by the prophets,
> Giving them a partial picture of Your eternal plan.
But You spoke completely and finally through Your Son
> To Whom You have given everything,
> And through Whom You created the universe.

Your Son is the radiance of Your glory
>> And the exact representation of Your nature,
>> His power sustains all things.
After the Son provided forgiveness of sins,
>> He sat down at Your right hand in glory.

Lord, I bow at the feet of Your son Jesus
>> *To worship Him with my whole heart*
For all that He is and for all
>> *That He has accomplished for me.*

Jesus Is Better Than Angels

Hebrews 1:4-14

Your Son is much greater in superiority over the angels,
>> His name—Jesus Savior—is much greater than theirs.
You never said to the angels, "You are my son,
>> In eternal day I have become Your Father."
You never said about the angels, "I am His Father,
>> He will be My son."
You said, "When I bring the First Born
>> Into the world, let all the angels worship Him."
You said, "I make the angels swift as the wind,
>> And my servants will punish with fire."
But about the Son You said, "Your kingdom, O God, will
>> Last forever and ever, and You will rule in righteousness;
>> You love righteousness and hate iniquity."
"Therefore, Your throne—Jesus—is set above all others,
>> And I—the Father—will pour out the oil of righteousness on You."
You called Your Son—Lord—when you said, "In the beginning,
>> O Lord, You laid the foundation of the earth;
>> The heavens were the work of Your hand."
"The heavens will vanish, but You—My Son—remain;

They will wear out like old clothes
But You—My Son—will remain forever
And Your years will never end."
You never said to any angel, "Sit at My right hand
Until I humble your enemies under your feet."
No, You didn't exalt any angel because they are spirits
Who minister to You in worship,
And they minister service to those who will receive salvation.

Amen

First Warning Against Neglect

Hebrews 2:1-4

Lord, I will pay careful attention to the biblical things I've heard
So that I don't drift away from You.
Because the message spoken by angels was true,
And every disobedience has its own judgment,
No one will go unpunished if they neglect
Your salvation that is promised to them.
The promise was first announced by Jesus Himself
And passed on to us by them who heard him speak.
God confirmed this message with signs, miracles
And gifts of the Holy Spirit distributed to them.

Christ Is Better Than Created Man

Hebrews 2:5-18

Lord, You did not make angels rulers of the world to come;
But You made Your Son ruler of everything.
David said in Psalms, "What is man that You are concerned about Him,
But you honor the Son of Man?"

"You made him a little lower than angels,
     So You could crown Him with glory and honor
     And You put everything under His feet."
"You left nothing that was not put under Your Son,
     Yet at the present time, everything is not subject to Him."
We see Jesus who for a short time was made lower than the angels,
     Now He is crowned with glory and splendor in Heaven,
Because by Your grace He submitted to death for all mankind.

Lord, it was Your purpose to allow Christ to suffer,
     Because through His death Jesus brought many to Heaven
     Becoming the leader of their salvation by His sufferings.
We have been made holy by Jesus, we have the same Father,
     And Jesus is not ashamed to call me His brother.
For Jesus predicted in Psalms, "I will tell my brothers
     About the Father and in their presence I will praise Him."
At another place Jesus predicatively said, "I will trust my Father;"
     And again He said, "Here I am with Your children
     You have given me."
Since all your human children have flesh and blood,
     Jesus shared this same humanity, so that by death,
He could destroy the one who holds the power of death
     That is the devil, and free all those held captive
     By the fear of death for their entire life.

Lord, Jesus didn't come to free angels, but to free humanity;
     For this reason Jesus became flesh like His brethren
     So He could become my merciful and faithful High Priest.
Now Jesus has made atonement for my sins,
     Because He Himself was tempted and suffered,
     Now He is wonderfully able to help me when I am tempted.

Amen

Jesus Is Better Than Moses

Hebrews 3:1-6

Lord, because You have set me apart for Christ,
  And because You have chosen me by a heavenly calling,
You want me to fix my thoughts on Jesus
  The Apostle and High Priest of my faith.
Jesus faithfully served You as a priest
  Just as Moses faithfully served You in the Holy Sanctuary;
But Jesus was worthy of greater honor than Moses,
  Just as the builder has greater honor than the house he built.
Every house is built by someone,
  But You are the builder of everything.
Moses was faithful to serve in Your House,
  His work was a type—illustration—of Christ's work that was coming,
But Christ has complete authority over Your House,
  And as a Christian, I am part of Your House
  So I will cling with confidence to that hope to the end.

Second Warning Against Unbelief

Hebrews 3:7-19

Lord, when I hear Your voice speaking to me,
  I will not stubbornly resist You as Israel rebelled against You and
  Wandered 40 years in the desert.
In the desert Israel constantly tested You and disobeyed You,
  Even though they knew what You did in the past for them.
That is why You were angry with them and said,
  "Their hearts are hardened and they refuse to obey Me,
  They shall never enter in the rest I have for them."
Lord, I do not have a disobedient heart that rejects You,
  I will listen to Your Word today so I won't develop

An unbelieving stubborn heart.
I will faithfully trust You to the end,
>   Just as when I was first saved
>   So I can share all the blessings You have planned for me.
But now, I will not harden my heart
>   As Israel did in the desert.

The Jews were the people who heard Your voice and rebelled?
>   They were the ones Moses delivered out of Egypt.
They were those who made You angry
>   So You made them wander in the desert 40 years
>   Because of their sin. Their bodies were buried in the wilderness.
Those were the ones You swore would never enter Your rest;
>   Why couldn't they enter the promised land?
>   It was because of their unbelief.

>   Amen

Jesus Is Better Than the Sabbath

Hebrews 4:1-16

Lord, since Your promise of entering Your rest still stands
>   I will be careful not to neglect entering Your rest.
You had the Gospel preached to me just as it was preached to Israel
>   But they couldn't take advantage of it because of unbelief.
Now, I can enter Your rest by faith, because You said,
>   "I made an oath that those who will not believe Me,
>   Cannot enter My rest."
I know Your rest is waiting for me because I will finish my work;
>   After You worked six days, You rested on the seventh day
>   Because You finished all Your work.
The promise remains for some to enter your rest today, even though
>   Those who heard the Gospel preached to them rejected it.

God still warns through the words of David, "Today,
> If you hear God's voice, do not harden Your hearts against Him."

If the promised rest was the land into which Joshua led them,
> God would not have later promised a different rest;
> Therefore, there remains a Sabbath-rest for You who read this letter.
When you enter your rest, you cease from your labor,
> Just as You—the Father—ceased from Your labor.
Therefore, I will make every effort to enter Your rest
> Being careful not to disobey You
> As the children of Israel did in the wilderness.

Lord, Your Word is alive and active, sharper than a two-edged sword,
> Piercing the unseen things such as my soul and spirit,
> Exposing my thoughts and attitudes for what they are.
Lord, You know everything about everyone,
> Nothing is hidden to You who will judge everyone,
> So You know who will enter Your rest.

Lord, Jesus Your Son has gone to Heaven as my great High Priest,
> So I will hold fast to my faith.
My High Priest understands me and sympathizes with my weaknesses
> Because He was tempted in all parts of His being, just as I am,
> Yet He did not commit sin.
So, I will come boldly to Your throne;
> So I will receive mercy and find grace in my hour of need.

Amen

Jesus Is Better Than Human Priest

Hebrews 5:1-10

Lord, the human High Priest was selected from among human men,
> And was chosen to represent Your people before You.

He sympathized with the ignorant and those who make mistakes
> Because as a mortal, the High Priest was subject to weaknesses.

This is why the High Priest offered sacrifices for his own sins
> Before he offered for anyone else.

No one makes a choice to be a High Priest,
> He must be chosen by God, just as Aaron was chosen.

So Christ did not make the choice to be the High Priest
> But You Father chose Him saying, "You are My Son,
> Today I have become Your Father."

Again You Father said, "You are a priest forever
> In the priestly order of Melchizedek."

In His earthly days Jesus prayed with loud cries and tears
> To You who could save Him from death;
> He was heard because of His obedience.

Although Jesus was Your Son, He learned what obedience was like,
> When he experienced suffering.

It was after this experience that Jesus became
> The giver of eternal life to those who obey Him.

Then You declared Jesus to be the High Priest
> After the order of Melchizedek.

Amen

Third Warning Against Disobedience

Hebrews 5:11–6:12

The author had a lot more to say about the priesthood of Melchizedek,
> But the readers didn't fully understand what he wrote.

When they ought to be teachers, they were still students;
> Needing someone to teach them the elementary truths of Christianity
> They needed milk, not solid food!

Spiritual babies still live on milk, not knowing how to live right because

Solid food is for mature Christians
Who by training can distinguish between good and evil.

Amen

Third Warning About Disobedience (Continued)

Hebrews 6:1-12

Lord, I won't stay with the elementary teachings about salvation,
But I'll go on to maturity in Christ.
I won't go back to my original repentance from sin,
Nor will I keep studying my baptism, or my spiritual gifts,
Or the resurrection from the dead, or eternal judgment.
Lord, I will build my life on these foundational truths
And grow to maturity in my daily walk with You.

It's impossible for those who are saved to go back to
The Temple to have their sins forgiven by a blood sacrifice.
If a person knew Jesus Christ, and tasted the heavenly gift,
And been filled with the Holy Spirit, and understood the Scriptures,
And felt the assurance of Heaven, and they turn against You,
It's impossible to be spiritually renewed in the Temple;
When they sacrifice a lamb, it's like crucifying again
The Son of God and torturing Him anew.

When farmland drinks in the rain from Heaven,
It grows a good crop because it experiences Your blessing;
That's a picture of our spiritual prosperity from You.
But if farmland keeps growing weeds and briers,
The land is worthless, and it might as well be cursed;
That's a picture of a person who doesn't produce spiritual fruit.
Even though the writer warns the readers,
He thinks they will do better things for You.
Lord, You are not unjust, You'll not forget a person's faith,

Nor his love, nor their good works.
I will show the same diligence to the very end of life,
>So I will get my full reward when I get to Heaven.
I will not become lazy, but will follow the example of those
>Who through faith and patience received the prize.

Amen

Jesus Is Better Than Abraham

Hebrews 6:13-20

I know You will do what You promised.
>When you made a promise to Abraham,
>Since You couldn't swear by any other, You swore by Yourself.
You promised to bless Abraham and give him many descendants;
>So Abraham received a son after waiting patiently for many years.
People today swear an oath by someone greater than themselves
>To guarantee what they promise and end all arguments.
Because You wanted to make it very clear to Your children
>What You would do, You guaranteed it with Your oath.
Lord, You have given me two things: Your promise and Your oath;
>Since it's impossible for You to lie, I know
>Without a doubt that I'll receive eternal life that You've promised.
I have this certain hope of Heaven as an anchor of the soul
>For I'm connected to Christ who has gone before me,
To enter the Holy of Holies in Heaven, where
>He intercedes for me as my High Priest.

Amen

Jesus Is Better Than Melchizedek

Hebrews 7:1-10

Lord, Jesus became a priest after the order of Melchizedek,
>Who was King of Salem and Your priest;
>He called You by the name El Elyon, Possessor of Heaven and earth.

When Abraham returned home after defeating the Kings,
>Melchizedek interceded for him. Then Abraham gave
>Melchizedek a tenth of everything he gained.

The name Melchizedek means King of Righteousness, and
>The title King of Salem means King of Peace.

There is no record he had any previous ancestors, or that he died;
>He is like the Son of God, a priest forever.

Lord, Melchizedek was great, even Abraham, the Father of the Jews,
>Gave him a tenth of all he had.

The Old Testament required the descendents of Levi who became priests
>To collect a tenth from all the people, i.e., their brothers.

However, Melchizedek did not trace his heritage to Levi, yet
>He collected a tenth from Abraham and blessed him;
>The one who has power to bless is the greater.

In the case of Levi, ordinary mortals received tithes
>But Melchizedek who received tithes, lives forever.

Levi who was in the body of Abraham paid tithes
>To Melchizedek who lives forever.

Therefore the Jewish priests who came from the rank of Levi
>Couldn't save us, God sent us Christ as a priest
>From the rank of Melchizedek to save us.

Amen

Jesus Is Better Than Aaron

Hebrews 7:11–8:5

For there to be a change of priesthood, there also
> Needed to be a change of law. Jesus who became a Priest,
> Was from the tribe of Judah, not from the tribe of Levi.

Moses didn't write anything about a person from Judah
> serving as a priest at the altar. So God's method
> Changed because Christ new position asHigh Priest
> Came from Melchizedek.

Christ didn't become a priest based on the requirements of Levi,
> Christ became a priest by the power of a life lived forever.

The Psalmist proved this about Christ, "You are a priest forever,
> After the rank of Melchizedek."

The former laws of priesthood were set aside because
> They were weak and useless. The law never saved anyone
> But now we approach God with a better hope.

God promised that Christ would be an eternal priest; remember,
> God never promised this about the Levitical priest.

Only to Christ did the Father swear, "You are a Priest forever
> After the rank of Melchizedek." Because of this oath
> Jesus now guarantees us a new and better covenant with God.

Under the old system, there were many new priests who took the place
> Of the older ones who died off.

But Jesus lives forever, and has a continuous priesthood,
> So I can come to You anytime through Jesus my intercessor.

Now Jesus is able to completely save me when I come to You,
> Since He lives forever to make intercession for me.

Lord, Jesus is the kind of High Priest I need,
> One who is holy, blameless and without sin
> And He has access to You in Heaven.

Jesus is not like human priests who need to sacrifice for their sins,
> First for Himself, then for others.

Jesus sacrificed only once for all the sins of the world
>When He once and for all offered Himself on the Cross.

The old law brought sinful men into the priesthood
>But your oath brought Jesus into His priesthood;
>He is my eternally perfect priest.

Amen

Jesus Is Better Than Aaron (Continued)

Hebrews 8:1-5

Lord, the writer makes the point that I have a High Priest
>Who sat down at Your right hand in Heaven,
>Who now serves in the heavenly Tabernacle that You set up.

Since earthly priests appointed by You offer gifts and sacrifices,
>Christ also must make offerings for sin,
>But His sacrifices are far better than the Levitical sacrifices.

Earthly priests serve in an earthly Tabernacle
>That is a reflection of the one in Heaven,

Because when Moses built the Tabernacle, You told him
>To build it after the pattern You showed him on the Mount.

Amen

Jesus Is Better Than the Old Covenant

Hebrews 8:6-13

But the ministry of Christ is far better than the former priest
>Because the new covenant is far better than the old one,
>Because the new covenant is based on better promises.

If there was nothing wrong with the old covenant,
>There wouldn't have been a need for a new one.

But You realized the old covenant was limited, so You said,
    "The day will come when I will make a new covenant
    With the people of Israel and Judah."
"It will not be like the old covenant I made with them
    When I led them out of Egypt."
"Israel did not keep their part of the covenant, so You cancelled it;
    You promised to write the new covenant in their hearts
    So they will know what You want them to do as Your people."
"No longer will people evangelize others saying, 'Know the Lord,'
    For all will know You, from the influential to the least important.
You promised to forgive their transgressions
    And no longer remember their sins."
Because You called this covenant "new," You made the old covenant obsolete;
    And what is old becomes antiquated and disappears.

Amen

Jesus Is Better Than the Old Sanctuary

Hebrews 9:1-10

Lord, the old covenant had laws about how to worship
    And its place to worship was a tent.
Inside this sanctuary were two rooms. The first room, called the Holy Place,
    Had the golden candlestick and a table of sacred loaves of bread.
Then there was the golden altar of incense
    That represents prayer, and a curtain that separates the two rooms.
The second room was called the Holy of Holies
    With the Ark of the Covenant, a gold covered chest,
    Which contained a jar with some manna, Aaron's rod that budded,
    And a stone engraved with the Ten Commandments.
On each end of the Ark were carved gold cherubim
    With their wings stretched out over the lid of the Ark
    Called the mercy seat, the place atonement was made.

Many priests followed certain regulations, going into the
      Outer room—the Holy Place—to carry out worship.
Only the High Priest entered the Holy of Holies, only once a year;
      He took blood with him for his and others' sins.
The Holy Spirit tells us by this illustration that the average person
      Could not enter the Holy of Holies
      As long as the old system of law was in place.
Lord, this illustration is important, because under the old system of law
      The sacrifices and gifts had to be continually given,
Because they never permanently cleansed
      The hearts of the worshipers.
The old system of laws dealt with what foods to eat,
      How to wash, rules about a lot of little things
      That people had to obey until Christ brought in a better covenant.

Jesus Is Better Than the Old Sacrifices

Hebrews 9:11–10:25

Christ came as the High Priest of a new and better covenant;
      He took blood into the Holy of Holies in Heaven and
      Sprinkled blood on the mercy seat to permanently forgive all sins.
Christ did not take the blood of bulls and calves into Heaven's
      Holy of Holies, but with His own blood He entered once and for all,
      To obtain eternal redemption for all who believe.
If the blood of bulls and calves could temporarily and outwardly cleanse
      Those who were unclean, thus sanctifying them,
How much more will the blood of Christ offered by the Holy Spirit
      Cleanse us, so we can serve the living God?
Therefore, Christ offered this new covenant to all, so that
      They may receive the promise of an eternal inheritance.
And don't forget Christ's death took away all the sins committed
      Under the old system of law.

When a person dies and leaves a will that is in question,
>The death of the one who wrote the will must be established;
>Then people receive the things that were promised in the will.
Therefore, the first system of law became operational when Moses
>Took blood and sprinkled everything having to do with the old law
>Saying, "This blood seals the agreement between you and God."
Moses then sprinkled blood on the Tabernacle and all
>The instruments of worship. All things were sanctified by blood,
>And without the shedding of blood, there was no redemption.
The tabernacle and instruments of worship are copies
>Of the true Tabernacle in Heaven. They were purified
>With the blood of animals.
But the Tabernacle in Heaven was purified with a better sacrifice;
>For Christ did not go into the earthly Tabernacle which is
>A copy of the heavenly one; He appeared before the Father for us.
Christ did not offer Himself repeatedly as the earthly
>High Priest does for himself and others. No!
Christ offered Himself once for all to do away with all our sin,
>And He did away with the existence of the first system of law.

Lord, I know it is appointed unto all people to die once,
>*Then comes the judgment.*
So Christ came once and took the sins of many;
>*The next time He comes to all those who wait for Him.*

Amen

Jesus Is Better Than the Old Sacrifices (Continued)

Hebrews 10:1-25

Lord, I know the old system of law was only a reflection
>Of coming spiritual realities, not the realities themselves.
The law could never bring the worshiper to spiritual maturity,

Even though repeated endlessly, year after year.
If the sacrifices sanctified the worshiper, or made him mature;
    Then they would have stopped bringing their sacrifices
    When they reached perfection.
Instead, the worshiper had to recall their sin yearly,
    Every time they brought a sacrifice, because
    The blood of bulls and goats never took away sin.
Lord, when Christ came into the world, He said,
    "Sacrifices and offerings didn't do away with sin,
    So You Lord, prepared a body for Me."
It is written in Scripture, "Christ has come
    To lay down His body as a sacrifice for sin."
And the Scriptures said of Christ, "I am here,
    I have come to do the Father's will."
By His death the Father cancelled the old system of law
    To establish a new covenant, a new system of law;
Under the new, we have been made pure and clean
    By the death of Christ, Who died for all, once and for all.
Under the old law, the priest had to offer the same kind of sacrifice
    Day after day, which never took away sin.
But Christ our priest offered one sacrifice for all time,
    To take away all sin,
    Then sat down at Your right hand in Heaven.
Now Christ is waiting for His enemies
    To become His footstool.
For by one sacrifice, Christ made those perfect
    Who claim the power of the Holy Spirit to live holy lives.
You said, "This is the new arrangement I will make
    After they have not kept the old system of law;
I will put My laws in their hearts
    So they will want to obey Me."
Then You said, "I will no longer remember their sins and lawlessness
    Because I have forgiven all sin,

There is no longer need of daily animal sacrifice."
Therefore, children of God, let us walk right into
    The Holy of Holies into the presence of the Father
    By the blood of Jesus Christ.
We have a new and living way into the Father's presence,
    Through the offering of Christ's body
    Which tore the curtain down.

Lord, I will come to You with a sincere heart,
    In full assurance of faith, having my life
    Sprinkled clean from a guilty conscience,
    And having been washed clean from sin.
Now I look forward with confidence
    To the hope of Heaven that You have promised me.
I will motivate others to a response of love and good works
    And I will meet regularly in the church,
    And encourage others who don't come, to be faithful in attendance
    Because the day of judgment is coming.

Amen

Fourth Warning Against Rejection

Hebrews 10:26-39

Lord, if anyone sin after they have been given knowledge
    Of the truth of the new covenant,
    There is no forgiveness in the animal sacrifice of the Temple.
They have only the terrible judgment of God to face
    And His raging fire that will punish rebels.
If those who rejected the law of Moses were killed without mercy,
    How much more severely will those be punished
    Who trample under foot the Son of God,
And considered His blood of the new covenant as unworthy

And insulted the Spirit of God who worked in their hearts.
Lord, You said, "Punishment belongs to Me,"
    So I know, "You will repay."
Also the Scripture said, "Because the Lord will judge His people;
    It is a fearful thing
    To fall into the hands of the living God.

Lord, I know many have suffered when they first believed;
    They stood for You in the face of insults and violence.
And sometimes they suffered because they stood with other believers
    Who were being persecuted.
They not only were persecuted because they stood with those in prison,
    But their goods were confiscated,
    Yet they knew they had better possessions in Heaven.
Lord, I will not let my confidence die away,
    Knowing I will be richly rewarded.
I will persevere, so that when I have done Your will,
    I will receive what You have promised.
Lord, I know in a little while, You will come
    And not be delayed.
I will do what the Scripture says, "The just will live by faith
    And if he shrinks back, You will have no pleasure in him."
Lord, I have never turned back from following You;
    No, my faith assures me that my soul will be saved.

Amen

The Superiority of Faith in Jesus

Hebrews 11:1–12:2

Lord, because of my faith I am sure You will answer my request,
    And my faith makes me certain about the things I can't see.
Because of my faith, I know the world was created by You

So that things seen came from things not seen.
Because of Abel's faith he brought a better offering
    Than did his brother Cain, and Abel pleased You.
You accepted Abel by receiving his sacrifice,
        And I can learn lessons of faith from Abel,
        Even though he is dead.
Because of Enoch's faith, You took him to Heaven without dying;
        No one could find him for You took him away
        Because You were pleased with him.

Lord, I know I can't please You without faith,
        So I come to You because I know You exist
        And I know You reward those who earnestly seek You.
Because of Noah's faith, he warned people about a flood
        He had never seen. Then he built a boat to save his family.
The faith of Noah condemned the world,
        And his faith gave him a basis to claim Your righteousness.
Because of Abraham's faith, he obeyed Your call
        When he left his home to go where You led him,
        Even though he didn't know where he was going.
Because of his faith, Abraham settled down in the Promised Land
        Like a stranger in a foreign country,
        Living in tents as did Isaac and Jacob who were heirs with him.
Because of his faith, Abraham confidently looked forward
        To living in a heavenly city that would be built by You.
Because of his faith, Abraham was able to become a father
        When he was too old to have children.
And Sarah, who was barren, had faith to bear a child,
        Because she realized that when You promised a son,
        You were certainly able to do what You said.
So the whole nation of Israel came from Abraham,
        When he was too old to have a child.
The nation of Israel had so many children
        That like the stars of Heaven, and the sands of the seashore,

They can't be counted.
Because of the faith of these people, they continued to look forward to
    The home You would provide for them,
Even though they never received it down on this earth;
    They confessed they were only visitors and strangers in this world.

Lord, when I agree with their faith, it means
    I too am looking for a heavenly city prepared for me.

Because of Abraham's faith, when he was tested,
    He offered up Isaac as a sacrifice to You.
Abraham believed Your promise that if he offered
    His only son as a sacrifice, You would
    Raise him from the dead,
Because You had promised, that from Isaac
    Would come the whole nation of Israel.
Because of Isaac's faith, he knew You would bless
    His two sons Jacob and Esau after his death.
Because of Jacob's faith, he blessed Joseph's two sons
    As he steadied himself with his staff to worship You.
Because of Joseph's faith, when he was about to die,
    He predicted the exodus of Israel from Egypt
    And instructed that his body be buried in the Promised Land.
Because of Moses' parent's faith, they hid him
    For three months after he was born
    Because they realized he was an extraordinary child.
Because of Moses' faith, he refused to be known as
    The son of Pharaoh's daughter.
Moses chose to suffer the affliction of Your people
    Rather than enjoy the pleasure of sin for a short time.
Moses considered that the "reproach of Christ"
    Was better than inheriting the riches of Egypt,
    Because he looked forward to the reward You would give him.
Because of Moses' faith, he left Egypt

And wasn't afraid of the King's anger;
>He would not turn back, because Moses saw You who are invisible.
Because of Moses' faith, he began the Passover,
>And sprinkled blood on the door post,
So the destroyer wouldn't touch the first born of Israel
>As the first born of Egypt died that night.
Because of faith, Israel walked through the Red Sea on dry ground
>But the Egyptians drowned when they tried to follow them.
Because of faith, Israel walked around the city of Jericho,
>And the walls fell down.
Because of the prostitute Rahab's faith, she received the spies
>And was not killed with the rest of the inhabitants.
There's more to be said about the faith of Gideon,
>Barak, Samson, Jephihah, Samuel, or David, or the prophets.
Because of the faith of these men, they conquered kingdoms,
>Did what was right, and received what You promised.
They were not harmed by lions, or the fiery furnace,
>And were protected in battle.
Some were given strength, to be brave in battle;
>They defeated foreign armies, and women received back their dead.
Others were tortured to death knowing they would
>Rise again from the dead to a better life.
Others were mocked, beaten with whips, chained in dungeons,
>Died by stoning, sawed in two, and put to death by the sword.
Some were homeless and wore skins of sheep and goats;
>They were destitute, and ill-treated,
>Living in deserts, caves, and ravines.
These were all heroes of faith, yet none of them
>Received their reward in this life.
God You have something better for them,
>But they must wait to share something even better with us.

Amen

The Superiority of Faith in Jesus (Continued)

Hebrews 12:1-2

Lord, I have this large crowd of witnesses watching me
    Therefore I will strip off everything that's in the way,
    Especially any sin that would trip me up.
And I will run steadily the race that I have begun
    Without losing sight of Jesus my leader
Who was willing to die a shameful death on the Cross
    Because He knew the joy that was coming in the future,
    And now He sits at Your right hand in Heaven.

Fifth Warning of Coming Punishment

Hebrews 12:3-17

When I think of the way Jesus endured such torture
    By sinful men for me, I will not give up.
After all, I've never had to take a stand for Christ
    To the point of shedding my blood.
I've not forgotten Your words of encouragement to me,
    "Do not be discouraged when the Lord rebukes you
    Or at His light chastening
Because the Lord disciplines those He loves,
    And punishes everyone He acknowledges as His child."
Lord, I know suffering is part of my training,
    Because You're treating me as Your child;
    What child is not corrected by their Father?
If anyone is not corrected by You, then they are not Your child,
    They are illegitimate children, and not Your true children.
Moreover, many have had wicked human fathers who corrected them,
    Therefore, I ought to be willing to submit to You—my
        heavenly Father.

My human father's punishment prepared me for life on earth,
>   But You are preparing me to live a holy life and for Heaven itself.
Punishment isn't enjoyable at the time I get it,
>   But it makes me live right and submit to the laws of men
>   So I will live in peace and develop character.
Therefore, I'll hold up under Your discipline,
>   So I'll not be weak, but strong.

Lord, I'll do everything possible to live peaceably with everyone,
>   And I'll live a holy life, because without it no one will see You.
I will make sure other believers don't miss Your grace,
>   And that no bitterness grows in the church
>   That causes trouble and poisons the assembly.
I will make sure no one is sexually immoral or ungodly
>   Like Esau who sold his inheritance for one meal.
Afterward Esau wanted his inheritance but was rejected
>   Even though he begged for it with tears.

Amen

The Presence of Jesus Is Better

Hebrews 12:18-24

Lord, we don't come to a mountain that burned with fire
>   To a religion that is dark and gloomy
>   To receive the first system of law, i.e., the old covenant.
We don't listen to a trumpet blast that was so scary
>   That the people begged it to stop.
We don't stay away from a mountain, "So that even if an animal
>   Touched the mountain, it had to be stoned."
The experience was so terrifying that Moses said,
>   "I am afraid" and he trembled with fear.

146

Lord, I come to Mount Zion, Your city, and the heavenly Jerusalem,
>   I come into Your holy presence
>   Where millions of angels gather to worship You.
I come with the church, right into Your city—heaven itself,
>   Where everyone is a first class citizen.
I come to You—Father—the judge of all people;
>   I join the spirits of all the redeemed who possess their inheritance.
I come to Jesus, the Mediator of the new covenant,
>   Whose blood intercedes better than Abel's sacrifice.

Sixth Warning of Future Judgment

Hebrews 12:25-29

Lord, I will never refuse to listen to You when You speak
>   As those who refused to listen to You and were punished.
How much more will those be punished
>   Who go back to Temple worship?
In the future You will send an earthquake to shake the earth;
>   You promised, "Once more I will send an earthquake,
>   Not to shake the earth only, but Heaven also."
Lord, this means at the final earthquake,
>   Everything will be removed that is not permanent;
>   Only the things made by You will remain.
Lord, I am part of the Kingdom that is unshakeable
>   Therefore, I will serve You with thankfulness.
I will worship You, but always with reverence and fear,
>   Because the fire of Your judgment always burns.

Amen

Faith in Jesus Is the Better Way

Hebrews 13:1-25

Lord, I will love Christians with brotherly love
  And I will be hospitable to strangers because
  Some have entertained angels without realizing it.
I will be concerned for those in prison, as though I were there,
  And I will remember those who are ill-treated
  Because I know how they feel.
I will honor the sanctity of the marriage vows
  Because the marriage bed should be kept pure;
  You will punish the adulterer and sexually immoral people.
I will live free from greedy lust for money,
  And be content with what I have. Because You promise,
"You will be my helper, I will not be afraid
  Of what anyone can do to me."

I will respect church leaders who teach the Word of God,
  I will remember their example and will imitate their godliness.
Lord, I rejoice that Jesus Christ is always the same,
  Yesterday, today and will continue forever.
I will not be side-tracked by strange new doctrines,
  I realize my spiritual strength comes from You, and
  I will not become godly by any rules I keep.
I am fed by the food that Christ gives me,
  No one can get spiritual strength by going back to the Temple;
  Those who do, won't be fed by Christ.
The bodies of animals whose blood is still used for sacrifice
  Were burned outside the city of Jerusalem,
So Jesus suffered outside the gate of Jerusalem
  To offer His blood for me and all who come to Him for salvation.
I will go to Him outside the Temple and outside the city walls,
  There to identify with Him, and bear His shame.

I realize there is no permanent city for me in this life,
      I look for an eternal city that will come in the future.
Therefore, I will offer my worship to You through Jesus;
      May my worship magnify Your name.
Also, I will continue to do good deeds and share with others
      Because You are pleased with that sacrifice.

Lord, I will continue to obey my church leaders and follow their directions
      Because they give an account to You
      Of how well they watch over my soul and others.
I will obey them so they will enjoy their ministry
      Because I would be the loser if I caused them grief.
I know that my conscience is clear in this matter,
      And I will act honorably in every way.

The writer asked for prayer that he could visit the readers,
      Now may You—the God of Peace—the One
      Who brought the Lord Jesus back from the dead,
      To become the Great Shepherd of the sheep,
Equip me thoroughly to do Your perfect will,
      By the blood of the everlasting covenant.
Lord, work in me everything that will please You;
      To Jesus Christ be glory forever and ever, Amen.

The writer asked the readers to listen patiently to this letter
      Because it is a short one.
He tells them Timothy has been released from prison
      And will come to see them;
      Also, he the writer will come with Timothy.
The Christians in Italy who are with the writer
      Send greetings to the readers.
Lord, I ask for Your grace and receive it by faith.

Amen

James

PRAYING THE BOOK OF JAMES
1:1–5:20

The Story of Writing the Book of James

James was a tall man with broad shoulders and big bones. His beard was now grey with age because he had endured many pressures as the elder of the church in Jerusalem. Beyond that he had seen much suffering by Christians in Jerusalem for the cause of Christ.

After Jesus was born to Mary, James was the next born to Mary; he was the legitimate son of Joseph, having been conceived by them and born a natural birth.

There came a time when Jesus left his boyhood home to begin his ministry by gathering disciples. James assumed the head of the household and gave direction to his brothers and sisters. Because James led the family, church leadership came natural to him.

After Jesus was raised from the dead, He appeared to James with a special message. No one knows what Jesus told His half-brother James, but James did become leader of the church in Jerusalem after that. It was that appearance that solidified James' fate so that he became unshakeable in all that he did. He was called "the just" and was an austere man with great legal understanding and a reverence for history.

James didn't spend a lot of time chatting with Christians and he was known as a man of few words. But he spent much time in prayer, so much time on his knees they developed huge calluses. He was nicknamed "old camel knees."

One thing James knew for sure, Christians were being persecuted all over the world. He heard quickly about the stoning death of Stephen and that he could be next. James knew that the head of the apostle James had been cut off and he could be next. He also knew that Saul, a young Pharisee from the Sanhedrin, had gone house to house arresting Christians, charging them before the Sanhedrin with crimes punishable by death. (That was before Paul's conversion.) Would he be imprisoned?

Because James had faced all types of persecution—real and imagined—he was qualified to encourage other believers who were facing sufferings. So James picked up a quill to write to Christians who were being persecuted for the cause of Christ, "Friends, don't be surprised if you suffer, as a matter of fact, rejoice in trials...."

Praying the Book of James

Preparing for Trials
James 1:1-27

Lord, James wrote a letter to Jews who were being persecuted
        And were scattered abroad outside the Holy Land;
        James wanted to prepare Christians everywhere for suffering.

Lord, I will rejoice when I suffer for You
        Even when I fall into every type of trial
        Because I know trials will build patience in me.
Lord, let patience have its perfect work in me
        That I may have complete faith, wanting nothing.
Lord, when I lack wisdom, I will ask You for it
        Because You liberally give us spiritual understanding
        And I know I will receive it from You.
But, I must ask with unwavering faith
        Because those who are unstable are like the
        Unpredictable waves of the ocean, driven by the wind.
The vacillating man will not receive anything from You
        Because a double-minded person is unstable in everything.

Lord, when I humble myself and take the low position,
        You will lift me up for Your purpose.

Those who exalt themselves as the rich shall be like
>The flower that is temporality here, then dies and is gone;
Because the sun burns them and they wither with the grass,
>Their beauty is destroyed in the same scorching heat.
>In the same way the proud will be destroyed.

Lord, bless me as I endure the trials that try me
>Because I will receive the crown of life for enduring persecution
>Which You have promised to those who continually love You.
When I am tempted to give up, I can't say You tempt me.
>For You do not tempt anyone to evil actions.
People are tempted by their own sinful desires
>That drag them away and entice them to sin.
When evil lust is planted and grown, it brings forth sin;
>And when sin is fully grown, it brings death.

Lord, I don't want to be deceived. I know every good gift
>Is from above; coming down from You, the Father of Light.
Lord, You give me spiritual birth through the word of truth
>That I might be a firstfruit of praise to Your glory.

Lord, I will be quick to listen, slow to speak,
>And even slower to become angry, because anger
>Does not produce a righteous life.
Therefore, I will get rid of all moral filth and
>Evil intent that is prevalent everywhere. I will
>Humbly accept the implanted Word which saves me.
I will not merely listen to the Word because that
>Is not enough. I will do what it says.
Those who merely listen to the Word and don't obey it
>Are like people who look at themselves in a mirror
>And forget what they see.
Lord, I want to look intently into the perfect law of liberty;
>I know You will bless me if I don't forget what I see there
>And I continue to obey what I learn there.

Lord, those who appear to be religious, but can't control their speech,
    Their religion is empty.
To have pure religion and be clean before You,
    I must minister to the needs of orphans and widows
    And keep myself unspotted from the world.

Lord, I've only had soft persecution in my life
    And I realize it's nothing compared to those who suffer terribly.
Help me to see Your presence and will in every uncomfortable situation;
    I will look for Your guiding hand in the sufferings of life.

Amen

Our Good Works Demonstrate Our Faith

James 2:1-26

My Lord Jesus Christ, I will not segregate myself for any person
    But will accept all people equally before You.
I will not show partiality to those who are rich, or finely dressed,
    Nor will I look down on those who are poor and dirty.
Lord, You will not bless those who accept only people in rich apparel
    And reject the poor by making them sit in a segregated place
    Or stand in the back of the crowd.
Those who show partiality are judged by their evil thoughts;
    I will accept all people equally, and
    I reject those who segregate themselves against any.
Lord, I know you love the poor of this world,
    Many of whom are rich in faith and heirs of Your Kingdom,
    Which you promise to all who love Jesus.
Those who despise the poor will eventually have some rich man
    Oppress them and deliver them to judgment.
These rich men blaspheme the very name of Christ,
    By whom all believers are called.

Lord, I will obey the second part of the royal law found in Scripture;
> I will love my neighbors as I love myself.

But if I reject anyone I am guilty of sin,
> And I have broken the Law.

If I keep the whole Law, but break just one point,
> I have broken all the Law.

Lord, you said "Do not commit adultery," and "Do not kill;"
> If I do not commit adultery, but I kill,
> Then I am a transgressor of the whole Law.

I will live by the Law, and speak it;
> Because I know I will be judged by it.

Lord, I know you will judge without mercy
> Those who have shown no mercy;
> But those who show mercy will persevere in judgment.

Lord, I know it is not good to minister by faith
> If I don't have good works to go with my faith.

If a brother or sister doesn't have bread and is naked,
> And I say go in peace be fed and be clothed,

But I do not give them what they need,
> What good is my faith?

Lord, if my faith doesn't result in good works,
> It is dead because it has no fruit.

If I tell anyone you have faith, and I have works,
> You will try to show me your faith without works
> And I will show you my faith by my works.

You can say that you have faith because you believe in God,
> That's all right, the devils believe in God but they tremble;
> You can't prove you have faith without works.

Lord, I realize our father Abraham was justified by works
> Which he demonstrated when he offered his son on an altar;
> Therefore, he demonstrated perfect faith by works.

Then the Scripture was fulfilled which said,

Abraham believed in God and it was counted to him as righteousness
Therefore, he was called a friend of God.
Now, I see how a person is justified by works,
Not by faith only.
Lord, I realize Rehab the harlot was justified by works,
Because she protected the Jewish messengers
And directed them away from the soldiers of Jericho.
Therefore, just as a body without a soul is dead,
So faith without works is also dead.

Lord, thank You for the deep faith You've put within me;
I'll serve You with all my heart
For I realize my deep faith is nothing
If good works don't automatically flow from my faith.

Amen

We Must Control Our Tongue

James 3:1-18

Lord, I don't want to be a teacher in position only
Because teachers are judged by a higher standard.
I know that I offend in many ways;
If anyone doesn't offend by their speech
They are perfect because when they control their mouth,
They control their whole body.
People put bits in horse's mouths to control them,
This is the way to turn around a horse.
A great ship is driven through the sea by fierce winds,
Yet they are turned around with a small rudder;
The ship goes wherever the captain decides.
In the same way, the tongue is a little thing
But it can boast great things and cause great trouble;

It's like a little flame that can start a great fire.
Therefore, my tongue can spread sin throughout my body
Just like a little flame can start a forest fire.
So my tongue can defile my entire life,
Not realizing it is a fire from hell.
People have been able to tame every kind of animal,
And birds and snakes, and things in the sea,
But no one is able to tame the tongue;
It is uncontrollably evil and deadly poison.
With my tongue I can bless You, even the Father,
Or I can curse people who are made in Your image.
Out of the same mouth comes blessings and curses, this is wrong;
Can a fountain give salt water and fresh water? Obviously not!
Can a fig tree produce olives? Obviously not!
Can an olive branch produce figs? Again no!
So I will not bless God and curse men!
If there is a wise man, I want to see his wisdom
In his conversation with other people;
I want to see his meekness and wisdom by the things he says.
Lord, those who are bitter, and envious and start arguments
Are full of self glory and they lie against the truth.
Their wisdom doesn't come from Heaven,
But comes from the earth, it is fleshly and devilish
Because they produce arguments, and confusion and evil.
Lord, give me the wisdom that is from above, it is pure,
Then peaceable, genteel, and will listen to others.
I want wisdom that is full of mercy and good fruits;
It doesn't have partiality to anyone
And it is not hypocritical.
Lord, I want the fruit of righteousness that is sown in peace;
I want to be a peacemaker.

Lord, I can discipline many areas of my life
But the most difficult to control is my tongue.

I know it's not the physical tongue itself, but my deceitful old nature;
Strengthen me to discipline my old nature so my tongue will
glorify You.

Amen

The Danger of Worldliness

James 4:1-17

Lord, I will not fight other believers, because these battles
Come from our old nature that makes Christians fight one another.
When I lust, I don't get what I want. People destroy others
And don't get what they want. People fight and argue
And still don't get the things they want.
I do not have what I pray for because I don't ask rightly,
Sometimes I ask and don't get what I request
Because I ask wrongly to satisfy my lust.

Lord, teach me the right things in life that I need,
Then help me to ask You for them in the right way.

Lord, you've told us that people who commit adultery
Are friends of the world and they hate You;
Help me realize those who are friends of the world are Your enemies.
Lord, I know the Holy Spirit in me has a strong desire
That I live a holy and godly life;
So let the Spirit give me more grace to repent of evil.
I know You said You give grace to those who humble themselves
But You resist the proud.
Lord, I will submit myself to You, I will resist the devil
So that he will flee from me and I'll have power from You.

Lord, I will not speak evil of other believers,
Those who say evil things about a believer

And judge a believer, actually hate the Law.
The Law prohibits me from judging one another
  And those who don't obey the Law actually hate the Law.

Lord, You are the only Lawgiver and I am accountable to You,
  You are able to free or judge, and You judge correctly;
  Take away all bitterness and give me love for all.

Lord, I will not say that tomorrow I'll go to a certain city
  And live there a year, buying and selling different things;
  That's because I don't know what will happen tomorrow.
What is my life? It is like steam from a kettle that's seen for
  A short time then it disappears.
Therefore, here is what I'll say, "If You will, I will live;
  And I'll do certain things within Your plan for my life."
"I will not take confidence in my boasting,
  Because boasting is evil;
  Since I know what good You want me to do, it's evil if I don't do it."

Amen

Because the Lord Is Coming—Pray

James 5:1-20

Lord, I know that all proud people will soon suffer misery,
  Therefore, they ought to weep and moan for coming judgment.
The riches they trusted in are corrupt
  And their fancy clothes are moth-eaten.
The tarnish on their gold is a witness against them;
  Their treasures will condemn them
  And their flesh shall be eaten with fire.
Lord, you hear the weeping of the workers who
  Harvest the field of the rich who defraud them.
The rich live in pleasure and fulfill their lust,

The rich condemn and "eat up" just people who do not resist them
But the rich have only fattened themselves for slaughter.
Lord, at the same time, the poor must be patient until You come,
Just as the farmer waits for his fruit to grow,
Waiting through the spring and fall rain,
So the poor must wait for Your coming judgment.
Lord, I'll not envy what other people have
Because You are the Judge standing at the door.
I will learn from the prophets who have spoken Your word;
They were blessed because they endured trials,
They are my example to teach me patience in suffering.

Lord, I have heard of the patience of Job and I know
What You do for those who endure suffering.
You are very tender and kind to them;
Lord, when I'm not patient, help me endure all my circumstances.

Lord, I will not swear in trials or pain
Neither by Heaven or earth;
I will let my *yes* be *yes* and my *no* mean *no!*
Because I don't want to be condemned by my speech.

Lord, I will pray when I am afflicted, and if I'm wrongly merry,
I'll read the Psalms to understand the severity of life.

When I am sick, I will call for the elders of the church
So they can pray over me and anoint me with oil in Your name.
I know the prayer of faith will save the sick
And You will raise them up.
If the sick will confess their sins, and pray one for another,
The sick will be healed and when they have committed sins,
They will be forgiven.

Lord, I know the continuous sincere prayer
Of a righteous man will accomplish much.
Elijah was a man subject to the same weakness as me,

But he prayed continually that it might not rain
And it didn't rain for three and a half years.
Elijah prayed again and You gave rain from Heaven
And the earth brought forth fruit.
Lord, if any believer strays from the truth and You restore him,
You not only turn around a sinner from his error
You save a soul from death
And hide a multitude of sins.

Lord, I try to pray but I'm not very effective;
I want to know the secret of power in prayer.
I know the secret is not in the mechanics of how I say it,
Nor is there power in my actual words I say,
Power is in You, and prayer is relationship with You.

Amen

First Peter

PRAYING THE BOOK OF FIRST PETER
1:1–5:14

THE STORY OF WRITING THE BOOK OF FIRST PETER

The shackles cut Peter's wrists as the Roman soldiers jerked him by the chains through the city gate leading away from Rome. It was then when Peter saw the terrible holocaust before his eyes. He saw hundreds of crosses and he heard the moans and cries of those being tortured, so Peter knew his fate. There were crosses on both sides of the road, stretching all the way to the top of the hill, almost a mile away. Hundreds of crosses...and on most of them were dead Christians left to rot in the Mediterranean sun with others still suffering. This was Rome's way of warning anyone not to become a Christian.

Peter knew his fate; he would be crucified like His Lord. He yelled back to his wife, also in shackles being pulled through the gate, "Keep the faith." But she couldn't hear him because of her torment.

Peter hoped that when they would crucify him their vengeance would be satisfied and somehow they would let his wife go. But the Romans had more torment for Peter than he imagined. Right there before his eyes he saw the soldiers slam his wife's body onto a cross, then callously nail her hands and feet in place. Peter had not seen the Roman soldiers nail the Lord to the cross, but he saw it in his heart. Peter closed his eyes as he heard,

"TWANG...TWANG...TWANG..."

As bad as this torture was, it was not the worse moment of his life. Peter thought back over 35 years ago on the night when he denied Jesus three times. Peter remembered the third time denying the Lord with curses. Just as he denied Him, the soldiers brought Jesus by. When Peter's eyes caught the eyes of Jesus, he was devastated. The worse moment in his life was failing the Lord.

And then Peter remembered that morning breakfast on the shore of Galilee. Jesus asked him three times, "Do you love Me more than these …?"[1] Peter had to confess that he hadn't loved the Lord with all his heart—again that was an embarrassing moment.

"Up she goes," the gruff Roman soldier grunted and the cross bearing Peter's wife was lifted high and dropped into its place. Another soldier grabbed Peter's head and forced him to watch. He knew that his wife would die shortly, she was a frail woman. He knew that she would go to be with Jesus. Even though his heart ached for his wife, Peter's soul was at peace.

"You, next," the Roman leader pointed to Peter with his whip, and to add to the pain, slapped him across the face.

"Not like my Lord," Peter appealed to the soldiers. "I don't want to die like Jesus died."

"Ha-ha," the Roman soldier laughed at him, "but you're gonna die."

"I'm not worthy to die like Jesus," Peter pleaded with the men, and then requested, "Crucify me upside down."

The soldiers laughed and then the leader said, "What an ingenious idea, you'll be tortured all the more." Immediately the soldiers began to make preparation to crucify Peter upside down. Peter was numb from all the torture he had endured, so he didn't feel the spikes; but he heard the sound.

"TWANG…TWANG…TWANG…"

It's as though Peter didn't feel the spikes tearing through his veins, and as though his feet were untouched. His mind was elsewhere. He was going to see Jesus.

"UP HE GOES," the leading soldiers yelled to the others, Peter was much heavier to lift into place than his wife. "This is it," Peter thought, "I'm going to finally die." Peter reviewed his service for Jesus Christ.

He remembered preaching the great sermon on the day of Pentecost. Peter boldly accused the Jews of crucifying his Lord and Savior. It was then when 3,000 were converted and baptized in one day.

Peter thought about the days he spent in Antioch, that great missionary church. It was there where he had great ministry with Paul; those were glorious days of usefulness.

And then Peter remembered preaching to the Jewish Christians throughout Asia Minor—today Turkey—where Christians were suffering for their faith. He was able to encourage them in persecution to remain faithful until death. Now on the cross, Peter was practicing what he preached to believers in trials.

And then Peter remembered the glorious days he preached in Babylon to the great groups of Christians in that city on the Euphrates River—what is today called modern Iraq. In Babylon there was a Synagogue where 10,000 Jews would gather, and Christians could fill it up when they came to worship the Lord Jesus Christ.

Young John Mark was with Peter in Babylon; it was there where the young disciple began writing the Gospel of Mark. Peter kept telling Mark things that he remembered that Jesus did, and said. Mark was writing the story of Jesus through Peter's eyes.

The agony of the crucifixion tore away at Peter's conscience. The sun was unrelenting, soon he would pass out. "Come, Jesus," Peter breathed an inward prayer, "come back to earth to establish Your Kingdom now…if not, Lord, receive my soul into Paradise." And with that prayer, Peter died.

As Peter stepped from the world of consciousness into the valley of the shadow of death, Jesus met him. The Twenty-third Psalm had promised, "Yea, though I walk through the valley of the shadow of death…You are with me" (Ps. 23:4). So Peter passed from earthly life into eternal life to be with the Lord forever.

Endnote

1. John 21:15

Your Full Salvation

1 Peter 1:1-25

Lord, Peter the apostle of Jesus Christ wrote a letter
>   To Jewish Christians who were scattered throughout Turkey
>   And to me who was chosen by Your foreknowledge.
Lord, I have also been sanctified by the Holy Spirit,
>   And cleansed by the blood of Jesus Christ.
May I obey You in every thought and action,
>   And enjoy Your grace and peace more and more.

Lord, I praise You, the God and Father of my Lord Jesus Christ,
>   Because in Your great mercy I was born again into your family;
>   I was given life by the resurrection of Jesus Christ.
Now may I have confidence in my perfect inheritance,
>   Reserved in Heaven for me that will not decay or change.
Through faith I am guarded by Your power
>   Until the coming of Your complete salvation
>   That will be revealed by Jesus Christ in the last day.
So I am truly glad this wonderful hope is ahead
>   Because I may have to suffer all kinds of trials on earth.
I know that when Jesus Christ is revealed, my faith, though tested,
>   Will be genuine like gold, and bring praise, and glory to You
>   When Jesus Christ returns to earth.
I love Christ even though I have never seen Him with my eyes;
>   Though not seeing Him I trust Him more because
>   He has filled me with joy that can only come from You.
I know my future reward for trusting Christ
>   Will be the salvation of my soul in the final day.

Lord, even the prophets didn't fully understand this salvation
    Even though they wrote about it;
    They had many questions about the meaning of Scripture.
They didn't understand what Your Spirit within them was saying
    When they wrote the prediction of the coming suffering of Christ,
    And they wrote of the glory that He would have afterward.
The prophets were told these events would not happen in their lifetime,
    But would occur many years later.
Now Lord, these events have happened and have been communicated
to all of us
    By those who have preached the Gospel to us;
    Now the angels, like us, have studied these predictions to know
Your plan.
Therefore, I will not let my thinking be sidetracked,
    Nor will I live in the future and ignore the present.
I will obey Your truth, and will not be conformed
    To the evil desires that controlled my life before I was saved.
I will live a holy life, just as You who called me to salvation is holy,
    Because the Bible says, "Be holy because God is holy."

Lord, I know that You—my Heavenly Father—have no favorites,
    Therefore, I will pray boldly with reverence,
    Knowing You will judge all people fairly.
I know I was not redeemed with gold and silver that perishes,
    From my meaningless life before I was saved.
But I was redeemed with the precious blood of Christ
    Who was a sacrificial lamb without blemish or spot.
Lord, You chose Him before creation for this purpose,
    But only in time did You reveal Him to us.
Now I have new life because You raised Christ from the dead,
    And glorified Him. Now I have hope beyond the grave.
Therefore, I will separate myself from sin and obey Your truth,
    And I will love believers with all my heart.
I was born again to new life, not from earthly parents,

Who give physical life that will eventually die.
But I was born again to new life that will last for eternity,
    That comes from the Word of God.
Yes, I know our physical life will pass away as the grass;
    Grass withers, flowers die, but Your Word of God stands forever,
    I put my trust in this Word that was preached to me.

Lord, Peter tells me about the greatness of Your salvation;
    Take away my spiritual blindness; help me see all You've done for me,
    Then help me live daily for Your glory.

Amen

Live Holy Because of Christ's Death

1 Peter 2:1-25

Lord, I repent of all known sin in my life,
    I will not lie, slander anyone, or be jealous of them.
Like a newborn baby, I thirst for Your pure Word;
    I want to taste Your goodness
    So I can grow to the fullness of salvation.
Indeed, I come daily to Christ for spiritual strength,
    He's the Rock rejected by unsaved people,
    But chosen because He is precious to You, the Father.
Now I am a living stone that's building Your house,
    But I'm also a holy priest offering worship to You.
As You said in Scripture, "Behold, I lay in Zion,
    Christ as My precious cornerstone."
But Christ the primary cornerstone is a stumbling block to the unsaved,
    And a stone used in execution to those who reject Him,
    But I am not disappointed in the One whom I believe.
Now Lord, I am part of a chosen people, a royal priesthood,
    A dedicated citizen of Heaven, and one claimed by You.

You have set me apart to proclaim the triumphs of Christ
      Who has called me out of darkness into marvelous light.
I am part of the people of God—a saved Gentile—
      Who once was not Your particular people, but now I belong to You,
      Who was outside of Your mercy, but now I have mercy.

Lord, I will keep myself free from self-destructive passions
      Because I am a pilgrim in a foreign land.
I will behave honorably among unsaved people
      So they can see for themselves my good works;
So that when the day of judgment comes,
      They will remember the things they now criticize.

I will submit myself to human institutions for Your sake,
      And especially to the government
      Because they are Your representatives to punish lawbreakers.
Lord, it is Your will that my good testimony
      Silence what fools have said about You in ignorance.
I am a slave to no one except You; I'll live free
      And I'll never use my freedom as an excuse to sin.
I will respect everyone, and I love the church, and fear You,
      And I keep the laws of my government.

Lord, I realize Christian employees must be respectful and obedient
      To their bosses, not only when the bosses are kind to them,
      But also when the bosses are cruel and demanding.

There is a reward for putting up with undeserved punishment
      When it is done for Christ's sake.
But there is no Christian reward when I'm punished
      Because I've done something wrong and deserve punishment.
My reward comes when I accept punishment patiently
      And do my duty, even when I don't deserve punishment.
Because when Christ suffered undeservedly for me,
      He left me an example that I should follow His steps.

Christ did not threaten to get even when He was tortured,
>But committed Himself to You, the Father, who will judge rightly.
Christ suffered for my sins on the Cross
>So I could repent of my sins and live a godly life;
>Through His wounds, I have been healed.
I was straying like a lost sheep, but now
>I have come back to the Shepherd and Protector of my soul.

Lord, Christ has provided a great salvation for me,
>*He makes me live holy as a saved person should live.*

Amen

The Sufferings of Christ

1 Peter 3:1-22

Lord, You tell a married woman to be obedient to her husband
>So that if he refuses to obey the Word of God,
He may be won to Christ by his wife's godly behavior
>Because her holy life speaks louder than her words.
You tell women not to dress up to show off,
>And they should not try to be spiritual,
>Depending on jewelry, lovely clothes and hair arrangement.
They must be beautiful inwardly, with a gentile spirit
>And a quiet appearance, which is what You want.
That kind of inward beauty was seen in women of the past
>Who trusted You and submitted to their husbands.
Sarah is an example who obeyed Abraham, calling him Lord;
>Women today can become her descendent by doing what is right
>And not worrying their husbands or giving them anxiety.

Lord, you tell husbands to treat their wives with respect
>And honor them as the weaker vessel,

Because husband and wife are heirs together of the grace of life;
>   When the husband does this, his prayers will not be hindered.

Lord, I will live in harmony with other believers,
>   I will be sympathetic, love all believers, be compassionate and
>   humble.
Lord, I will never repay wrong with wrong, or a curse with a curse,
>   Instead, I will repay a curse with a blessing;
>   That is what You call me to do, and I will be blessed by You.
Lord, because I want a happy life and enjoy prosperity,
>   I will not let my tongue lie, and become deceitful.
I will turn away from evil and will do good;
>   I will try to live peaceably and hold on to it when I catch it,
Because You are watching me and listening to my prayers,
>   But You frown on those who do evil.

Usually no one tries to hurt me when I do good,
>   But if they do try to hurt me, You will reward me;
>   I will not be afraid of them or their threats.
I will hold the Lord Jesus reverently in my heart
>   And when someone asks why I believe as I do,
>   I'll tell them a reason for the hope I have in Christ.
But I'll give my answer with courtesy and respect
>   So that when attackers curse me, they will become ashamed
>   When they see my exemplary life and conduct.
If it is Your will that I suffer,
>   It is better that I suffer for doing right instead of wrong.

Lord, thank You that Christ once suffered for my sins,
>   The just for the unjust, that He might bring me to You,
>   Being put to death in the flesh, but raised by the Spirit.
Christ descended into hell to preach to people in prison
>   Because they were disobedient to You and refused to repent,
Like those who rejected Noah's preaching, even when
>   You waited patiently while Noah was building the ark.

But only eight persons were saved from that terrible flood;
> The flood was a symbol of baptism; the water is a picture of
> > judgment;

It is a picture of the judgment for sin that Christ suffered on the Cross,
> Whereby we received cleansing for our sins by His death.

And we received the promise of eternal life because Christ was resurrected;
> Then He entered Heaven to sit at God's right hand,
> And now angels and Heaven are subject to Him.

Lord, my suffering is nothing compared to what Christ suffered;
> *Now I have access to all spiritual blessing because of His death.*

Amen

Attitudes About Suffering

1 Peter 4:1-19

Lord, I know Christ suffered when He was tortured,
> Therefore I will also be ready to suffer for my faith;
> I will have the same attitude as Christ.

I will not suffer in my body because of personal sin,
> Therefore I won't let sin have domination over me;
> I will always do Your will.

I have lived too long to go back to my unsaved ways, giving myself to
> Sex, debauchery, drunkenness, orgies, and worshiping idols.

My unsaved friends think I'm strange for not indulging myself
> In the same evil activities that they do,
> They laugh at me in scorn.

But they will have to give account to You who judges the living and dead,
> Then they will be punished for the way they lived.

This is why the Gospel was preached to those who died in the flood;
> Their physical life suffered in the flood,
> But their spirits live so they will appear before You in judgment.

The world will soon come to an end, and

I will be clear-minded and self-disciplined so I can pray
> For all who don't know You and do Your will.
I will love everyone because love makes up for my faults;
> I will feed and give hospitality to those who need it.
You have given me special abilities; I will use them to help others,
> Being careful to pass on Your kindness.
If You call me to preach, I will allow You to speak though me;
> If You lead me to help others, I will do it in Your strength.
Lord, I want You to be glorified in my life through, Jesus Christ;
> To Christ be glory and power, forever and ever, Amen.

I will not be surprised when painful trials come,
> Because trials are not an unusual thing for Christians.
I will be glad that I can suffer as did Christ,
> Then I will rejoice when His glory is revealed.
When people curse and blaspheme me as a Christian,
> I will have Your blessing resting on me.
My suffering will not be for crimes such as murder or theft,
> Or even for sins, such as hurting people or gossiping.
When I suffer as a Christian, I will not be ashamed
> But will praise You that I bear Christ's name.
Time will come when judgment begins among God's followers,
> If I will be judged for my failures,
> How much more will the unsaved be judged?
If the righteous will barely make it through judgment,
> How much more punishment will the ungodly have?
So, when I suffer for doing Your will, I will keep doing right;
> I will trust my soul to You, the faithful Creator,
> For You will never fail me.

Lord, I'm not good with suffering,
> *And I don't like to be hurt physically or emotionally;*
> *But if I have to suffer for You, I will count it a privilege.*

Amen

Serving Christ in View of His Return

1 Peter 5:1-14

Lord, Peter spoke to church elders, because he was an elder,
> A witness of Christ's suffering, and one who will share in His glory.

Peter told elders to feed the flock that God has entrusted to them,
> Ministering as overseers, not because they must,
> But because they are willing to do what You want them to do.

Peter told them, "Don't do it for money, but serve eagerly;
> Don't be dictators over God's people, but be an example
> That everyone in the flock can follow."

"When the Chief Shepherd shall appear,
> They'll receive a Crown of Glory that will never tarnish."

Peter told the younger men to follow the leadership of the older men;
> The rest were to clothe themselves in humility but serve one
> > another;

Because You oppose the proud but give grace to the humble,
> Therefore, I will bow before You, so You can lift me up.

I will put the weight of all my problems on You,
> I will be watchful for attacks from my enemy, satan;
> He prowls as a hungry lion, looking for prey to feed upon.

I will stand firm against satan, knowing Christians throughout the world
> Are undergoing all types of suffering.

After I suffer for a while on this earth,
> You who have grace, will call me to an eternal glory of Christ.

But now You can protect me, make me stronger, and confirm me;
> To You be all power, forever and ever. Amen

I am encouraged to learn how you bless believers
> Who are going through the same kind of sufferings that try me;
> Therefore I will stand firm.

Peter sent this letter by Silas, whom he trusted;

The church in Babylon sent greetings along with Mark,
Greeting all believers in all peace;
Peace to all in Christ.

Lord, I never like to think about suffering,
But Peter reminds me that all Christians will have some suffering;
Help me suffer in Your will, to Your glory.

Amen

Second Peter

PRAYING THE BOOK OF SECOND PETER 1:1–3:18

THE STORY OF WRITING THE BOOK OF SECOND PETER

Simon Peter sat with several of his students as he taught them about Jesus Christ. He was describing the sermons of Jesus when a student spoke up, "There are teachers in the church that claim Jesus was not fully God." The student wanted to know how to answer those who said, "Jesus was a spirit from God, but not God Himself."

Then to prove to the students that Jesus was God, Peter described the transfiguration of Jesus on the mount, "No other person has ever been supernaturally changed so that His face shone like the sun and His garment sparkled."

Then Peter reinforced the point by adding he heard the Father speak from Heaven, "This is My beloved Son in whom I am well pleased."

The student answered Peter, "You must write that story in a book so we can answer those who teach false doctrine."

Peter nodded his head in agreement. The spreading grey covered his previous red hair. The twinkle in his eye told his students Peter was thinking how to answer them. Then Peter blurted out,

"I'll do it—I'll write a second epistle." Peter let his thoughts gush out, "I'll begin my second letter, 'Peter, a servant and apostle of Jesus Christ,' that way false teachers can't deny what I write. They must believe what I write."

Peter explained many of the false teachers were not children of God, "So I'll begin by explaining God has given us many precious promises in Scripture so we can receive a new divine nature—false teachers haven't been born again."

Then the eyes of Peter narrowed and the lines in his face hardened—not deep lines from fishing in stormy weather—but deep furrows that reflected his explosive temper. Peter's anger could erupt and boil over. "Those false teachers bring damnable heresies into the church. They're as despicable as the angels who were cast into hell, and as sexually corrupt as the homosexuals of Sodom and Gomorrah. Peter was angry because false teachers used false doctrine as an excuse for their shocking immorality. "I'll expose them," Peter's voice rose to emphasize his passion.

"And they don't think Jesus is coming back!" Peter told his students. "They mockingly asked—when is He coming?" Peter explained that his next epistle would show how false teachers would be punished at the second coming of Jesus Christ. Peter let a quiet smile overcome his anger, he reminded his students, "The Lord is not slack concerning His promises...."

Peter rose to leave his students, announcing, "I must begin immediately. I'll write a second epistle so each one of you will have an authoritative answer when false teachers raise foolish questions in the church."

With that, Peter abruptly left the room to begin writing. It fit his impetuous nature; every thought became an immediate action.

The students knew their teacher well. They knew that shortly Peter would emerge with a letter to protect the churches from heresy. Whereas Luke wrote from research, and Matthew wrote from a daily journal he kept of Jesus' action, Peter would pour out words from his fiery temperament, and his letter would rip the backs of false teachers like the punishing thongs of an executioner's whip.

Then Peter reminded his students that Jesus once asked him, "Who do you say that I am?" Peter's eyes twinkled, "It's the same answer—Jesus is our Messiah, the Son of the living God."

Praying the Book of Second Peter

Learning Virtue From the Scriptures

2 Peter 1:1-21

Lord, teach me to be as bold as Simon Peter
      Who wrote a letter addressed to Christians who
      Had obtained the same precious faith as he received.
Lord, I too have that precious faith and I stand
      In Your righteousness and of my Savior, Jesus Christ.
May Your grace and peace be multiplied in my life
      As I grow in knowing You and the Lord Jesus.
Your divine power has given me all things that relate
      To life and godliness, so I will grow as I
      Know You who called me to a life of excellence and goodness.

You have given me Your precious promises that
      Through the Word of God I have received a divine nature
      Which is the new man with new desires to obey You.
Therefore, I will add character to my faith
      So I will do the right thing in the right way.
I will add Bible knowledge to my character
      So I will always know what to do to please You.
I will add self-control to my biblical knowledge
      So I will be steadfast in knowing and doing right.
I will add godliness to my biblical knowledge
      So that I'll have a basis to become more godly.
Finally, I will add brotherly love to my godliness
      So that my godly life results in a loving relationship to all.
When I abound in these traits, I will not be
      Ineffective or unfruitful in my walk on this earth.
Those Christians who don't have these godly traits are blind,
      They have forgotten that their former sins are forgiven.

I have been called to salvation and chosen by You;
      I will give diligence to demonstrate Your call in my life.
If I do all these things, there is no danger
      That I will ever fall away into sin,
Then I will eventually be given admission to Your eternal Kingdom
      To live forever with my Lord and Savior, Jesus Christ.
Throughout eternity, You'll continually re-tell these truths to me,
      Even though I know them now and hold them firmly.

Peter said it is his duty to remind every one of these truths
      As long as he is in the body, i.e., the tent.
Peter knew his time to leave the tent was coming soon
      Just as the Lord Jesus predicted His death.
Therefore, Peter wrote these things so that after his departure,
      Believers everywhere would be able to recall these things.
Peter did not make up a myth when he
      Went preaching the power of the coming of the Lord Jesus Christ;
      Peter saw with his eyes the majesty of Jesus for himself.
Peter was on the Mount of Transfiguration when the Father spoke,
      "This is my beloved son, in whom I am well pleased;"
      Peter actually heard that voice with his ears.

Therefore, I hold more certain than ever the word of prophecy
      And I will give careful attention to that word
      For it shines like a bright light in a dark world.
It will shine until the day of Christ's return
      Which is the morning star arising in our hearts.

I understand and believe that no prophecy of Scripture
      Can be interpreted and understood in isolation,
      But every verse must be interpreted in light of the whole Scripture.
No word of prophecy was written by human initiative,
      Men who wrote the Bible were inspired
      By the Holy Spirit who wrote through them.

Lord, thank You for Your Word of God that saves me;
Help me to master the Scriptures, then meditate on them
And live a godly life that's taught therein.

Amen

Warning Concerning Apostasy

2 Peter 2:1-22

Lord, there were false prophets living when the Bible was written
    Just as there are false prophets today.
These false prophets will subtly introduce dangerous heresies,
    They will deny You Who redeemed them
    And eventually they will cause their own destruction.
Many will follow their filthy immorality,
    And by their lives discredit the truth of God.
In their lust, they will try to make many people their disciples
    But their foolish arguments make their judgment inevitable.
I know You didn't spare the angels that sinned
    But bound them in chains and threw them in hell,
    So they must wait for the judgment day.
And You didn't spare any of the people who lived before the flood;
    You completely destroyed the world with a flood
    Except Noah who spoke for You and his family of seven.

Later, You reduced the cities of Sodom and Gomorrah
    Into a heap of rubble and completely destroyed them
    As a fearful example to those who refuse to live by Your laws,
Yet, You saved Lot, and declared him righteous
    Even when he was distressed at the sin of his day.
Lot saw and experienced the filthy sins as he lived among sinners,
    And these sins tortured his soul day after day
Because You delivered Lot, I know for certain that You can

Rescue the righteous who are surrounded by temptation;
And I know that You reserve Your punishment
    For the wicked until the day of judgment comes.

Lord, I know Your judgment is reserved for those
    Who indulge in their lust and despise authority.
These are arrogant and presumptuous, they dare to
    Scoff at the Glorious One, the Lord Jesus Christ.
Even the angels who are more powerful than they,
    Never criticize these evil men before Your presence.
Lord, these evil men are as dumb as animals
    Which You gave us to eat and do our work;
    These men laugh at the great powers of the unseen world.
But they will be destroyed in their own corruption,
    They will be destroyed with satan and the demons in hell.
These men who do their evil in broad daylight are cancerous spots
    Who revel in sin even when they come to Your house to eat.
They look everywhere for adultery and seduce the unsuspecting;
    They are cursed because they magnify their greed.
They have left the right path to follow
    The path of Balaam who tried to profit from his sin.
The donkey rebuked Balaam with the voice of a man
    To restrain him from his sin.

False teachers are like wells without water,
    They are like storm clouds without rain;
    The dark underworld is reserved for them.
With their proud works they tempt new converts
    To return to sin, who have just escaped the world.
They use lust to coax new believers back into sin,
    They promise freedom, but they are slaves themselves
    Because they are dominated by sin.
Anyone who escapes the pollution of this world
    And allows themselves to be enslaved again,

His second state is worse than his first one;
> It would have been better if he never learned the way of holiness.

He is like the proverb that says, "The dog returns to his own vomit," and
> "A pig that is washed returns to wallow in the mire."

Lord, thank You for salvation and a new desire to serve You.
> *I never want to return to sin;*
> *I promise I will always follow You and live a godly life.*

Amen

The Return of Christ

2 Peter 3:1-18

Lord, Peter wrote this second letter, and in both letters
> He tried to motivate people to spiritual thinking

So they would remember the words of the prophets
> And keep the commandments of the apostles of the Lord Jesus Christ.

Peter wanted to remind them that scoffers would come
> In the last days following their own evil lust.

Scoffers will say, "Where is His coming?" They will add,
> "Ever since our fathers died, everything goes on as
> It has since the beginning of creation.

They deliberately close their eyes to the fact
> The earth was formed out of the waters by Your command.

They also forgot that the earth was covered by water
> And that the present Heaven and earth are being maintained by You,
> And that one day You will judge this earth by fire.

Lord, I believe You created all things and that you judged
> *The earth by water. I believe one day you will judge the*
> *World by fire. Help me live godly in light of Your coming.*

Lord, I will never forget that a day with You is a thousand years,
    And a thousand years is only a day.
I realize some people think You are slow about keeping Your promises,
    As some people measure slowness,
    You will keep Your promises in Your time.

Lord, I know You do not want anyone to perish
    But You want all people to repent and trust You for salvation.
Lord, You will come as a thief in the night
    When the heavens will pass away with a thunderous noise,
    And the elements will dissolve with fire,
    And the works on earth will be burned up with fire.
In view of all these things, I will live godly;
    I will live a good life, looking for Your return.
That is the day when the heavens will disintegrate with fire
    And all the elements will melt.
My hope is set on the new Heaven and new earth
    Which you have promised where the righteous will live.
I will wait in hope for these things, and be found in You
    Without blemish or spot at Your coming.
I know why You are waiting to return. You are giving us time
    To get this message of salvation to as many as possible.
    Paul wrote about these same things in his letters
    Yet some of his comments are not easy to understand.
    Some people who are unlearned and rebellious
    Deliberately have twisted his writings to mean
    Something quite different from what he meant,
Just as they do other Scriptures
    Which is disastrous to them.

Peter wrote to us about these false teachers so we can watch for them,
    And not be fooled by them,
    But that we may stand firm on biblical doctrine.

I will grow in grace and in the knowledge of the Lord Jesus Christ,
   To Him be all glory
   Both now and forever.

Amen

First John

PRAYING THE BOOK OF FIRST JOHN
1:1–5:21

THE STORY OF WRITING THE FIRST LETTER OF JOHN

The aged John saw heresy slipping into the early church. It stirred him to the depths of his soul. He decided to write a letter to the churches to warn them of false doctrine. John told his personal attendant Ansel,

"Many younger preachers don't realize that Jesus was fully man, yet fully God."

The old apostle explained that churches were being influenced with the philosophy of Greek gods. Just as their gods from Mount Olympus were half God and half human, some Christians ministers were preaching Jesus was half man and half God—an *eion*—somewhere between god and man, not fully God nor fully man.

John told Ansel, "I want to write a letter to be read to the churches so all believers will know the truth." This letter is what early Christians came to call *First John*.

Ansel said, "You must begin your letter with strong authority, like Paul began his letters." Then Ansel said that Paul began writing, "Paul, an apostle of Jesus Christ...." Ansel reminded that Paul's letters had the authority of an apostle. He suggested this letter should begin, "John, an apostle of Jesus Christ." That way everyone would pay attention to its message and believe it.

Old John shook his head negatively. "No," he said. He didn't want to begin egotistically or call attention to himself by using the introduction, "John, the apostle of Jesus Christ."

The old apostle knew everyone recognized he was an apostle, so he didn't have to say it.

Then Ansel said, "Begin the letter, 'From the apostle whom Jesus loved,' or 'The apostle who leaned his head on the breast of Jesus.'" Those were phrases John used to describe himself in the Gospel of John.

"No," was the simple answer of the beloved apostle. John had learned humility. He was a different man. He was no longer the fiery, young disciple who wanted to pray fire from Heaven on some listeners who would not receive Jesus. Jesus called young John "Son of Thunder" because his hot temper got him into trouble. In aged humility John didn't want to bring unnecessary attention to himself.

But young Ansel still argued, "How will they know this letter is from you?"

"Because I will send it by messenger to the church of Ephesus, and the messenger will tell them that I wrote it."

But Ansel still had a question. "The scribes of Ephesus will copy the letter, and it will be sent to all the other churches. Those reading the letter in other churches won't know it's you."

Old John beamed; his smiling wrinkled eyes reflected his ingenuity. "When people begin to read this letter, it will sound just like the introduction to the Gospel of John and everyone knows that I wrote that. So John began to write, "The Word existed from the beginning, we have heard it, we have seen it with our eyes and our hands have handled the Word of life...."

"There," John looked up from his writing to young Ansel, "doesn't that sound like me?" And then he pointed to the phrase, "From the beginning." "Readers will know this is the same way I began the Gospel of John."

Then John explained that Paul emphasized legal words in his letters, such as justified, adopted, pre-determined, and reconciled. Then John said, "The words I emphasize are different. I talk about family relationship and being children of God. I emphasize words like light, darkness,, abide and verily, verily." John smiled, "Everyone will know I wrote this letter by its vocabulary."

Fellowship With the Father Because of the
Incarnation of Christ

1 John 1:1-10

Lord, I have heard the message that is from the beginning,
      Which my spiritual eyes have seen and looked upon,
      And my hands have handled—the WORD OF LIFE.
Eternal life was manifested to me, I have seen it;
      And now I witness to others
      And tell them about eternal life
      Which was with You the Father, and manifested to me.
That which I've seen and heard, I tell others
      That they may have fellowship with me
      As I have fellowship with You,
      And with Your Son, Jesus Christ.

Lord, I worship You because You are light
      And there is absolutely no darkness in You;
      So now I declare this message to everyone.

Lord, if I tell people that I have fellowship with You
      Yet walk in darkness, I lie; and deny the truth.
But when I walk in the light as You are the light,
      I have fellowship with other believers, and the blood of Jesus Christ
      Cleanses me of all my sins.

Lord, if I tell people I have no sin in me,
      I deceive myself, and I don't have Your truth.
When I confess my sins, You are faithful
      To forgive my sins, and cleanse me from all unrighteous.
If I were to say I've never sinned one time,
      I make You a liar, and Your Word doesn't control me.

Lord, because of everything
  You've done for me,
  I'll love You and live for You.

Test of Fellowship With the Father

1 John 2:1-29

Lord, because You told me not to sin, I won't do it;
  But when I slip and sin once, Jesus Christ stands
  At Your right hand to plead forgiveness for me.
I know Jesus has forgiven all my sin
  And He didn't die for me alone, but for the whole world.
I have confidence that I'm Your child
  Because I keep Your commandments.
Those who say that they know You, but don't keep Your commandments,
  Are liars, and they don't have the truth.
But those who keep Your Word, have Your love in their hearts
  That's why I know I'm Your child.

Lord, John didn't write anything new in His letter
  He just repeated the original commandments You gave us,
  And that commandment is found in Your Word.
Then John added what is new about the old commandments;
  Those who claim to be in the light, but hate their brother,
  They are in darkness until now.
Those who love their brother live in Your light
  These persons will not stumble in darkness.
Lord, those who hate their brothers live in the darkness of sin,
  And walk in darkness and they don't know what they're doing,
  Because the darkness of sin has blinded their eyes.

Lord, John has written to new children in the faith
  To let them know their sins are forgiven.

Lord, John has written to those mature in the faith
    Because they have known You from the beginning.
Lord, John has written to young men because they
    Overcame the evil one.
Lord, John has written to children in the faith
    Because they know You.

Lord, I will not love worldly attractions, or anything else
    That will pull me away from You. Those who
    Love the world, do not love You, the Father.
Because worldly attraction involves the lust of the flesh,
    The lust of the eyes, and the pride of life,
    These are not from You, but are from the evil one.
I know the world will pass away, as well as fleshly lust,
    But I will live forever by doing Your will.

Lord, John has written that we live in the last days
    And that antichrist will come in the future. Because the
    Spirit of antichrist is already here, we know he will come.
Many Christians have stopped fellowshipping with us
    Which demonstrates they have abandoned their faith,
For if they were of us, they'd still fellowship with us;
    Because they went out from us proves they were not believers.
Lord, I have an anointing of the Holy Spirit
    So I can know spiritual things.
John wrote to us because we know the truth,
    And that no lie comes from the truth.
Those who deny that Jesus is the Messiah are liars,
    They have the spirit of antichrist because
    They deny both You the Father and the Son.
Those who deny the Son, don't have Your presence in their lives;
    And those like me, who have the Son,
    We also have You.
If I continue in the message I heard from the beginning,

And I continue fellowshipping with You and the Son,
   I have the promise of eternal life.
Lord, I still have the anointing you gave me at salvation,
   So I don't need anyone to explain truth to me.
That anointing gives me basic spiritual understanding
   So I will abide in the truth that has been taught me.
Lord, I know that Jesus Christ is righteous
   So all those who obey the truth taught by Him
   Are born of God.

Lord, thank You for giving me inward confidence
   That I have eternal life.

Amen

How Believers Relate to Each Other

1 John 3:1-24

I often think about the love of You—the Father—for me
      And the fact that You call me Your child
      Because I really belong to You.
When the world refuses to acknowledge You,
      It also refuses to recognize my salvation.
Yes, I am already Your child, and I can't imagine
      What our fellowship will be like in Heaven.
I do know this much about my future life,
      When Jesus comes, I'll be like Him
      Because I've seen Him in the Word of God.
Everyone who agrees with me about our future relationship
      Will keep themselves as pure as You are.

Anyone who keeps on sinning breaks Your commandments
      Because sin is breaking Your law.
I know Jesus became a man to take away sin

And that there is no sin in Him.
So when I stay close to Jesus, I won't be sinning
    And those who sin continually, were not saved
    In the first place and they don't know Him.
I am Your child, so I won't let anyone deceive me;
    I will live holy because You are holy.
Those who constantly sin belong to the devil;
    Sin began with the devil and he constantly keeps sinning.
I know the Son of God has come to undo all that
    The devil has corrupted with sin.
Because I have been born again, I don't constantly sin
    Because I have a new nature that tells me what to do.

This is how you tell the difference between a child of God
    And a child of the devil. Whoever constantly sins
    And doesn't love other Christians, is not in Your family.
I have heard Your message from the beginning
    That I am commanded to love other believers.
I will not be like Cain who killed his brother
    Because he was not your child,
    And I won't be surprised when the world hates me.
When I love other Christians, it proves I have been
    Delivered from death and hell and I have eternal life.
If I refuse to love a believer, it proves I am just the same as
    A murderer, and murderers don't have eternal life.
I know true love from the example of Jesus Christ,
    Because He died for me; I ought to live for others.
If someone has money and professes to know You,
    Yet refuses to give to a needy Christian,
    How could Your love live in Him?
Therefore, I will not love in words only,
    I will show my real love by the things I do.
Only by actions can I be sure that I am Your child,
    And my conscience will be clear when I come to Your presence.

When my conscience makes me feel guilty because I sin,
> I realize You know everything about me
> For You are greater than my conscience.

Therefore, when my conscience doesn't convict me,
> I can come to You with my request in prayer
> To get what I ask, because I am keeping your commandments.

And this is Your commandment that I believe
> In the name of Your son, Jesus Christ,
> And that I love believers as You commanded us.

Because I keep Your commandments, I know I live in You,
> And You live in me. The Holy Spirit gives me this assurance.

Lord, I want to love everyone more and more;
> *Help me love others, as You love me.*

Amen

Warning Against False Teachers

1 John 4:1-21

Lord, I will not believe every person who claims
> To be a Christian, but I will test their spirit

To see whether they are from You.
> Because many false teachers are going around.

Every spirit that acknowledges that Jesus Christ
> Has come in the flesh is from You;
> Every spirit that denies Jesus had a body is not from You.

Those who deny Jesus was human are antichrists, who
> Were predicted to come, and are now here.

If Jesus didn't come in a body, He couldn't live a perfect life,
> Nor could He have died, nor would He have bled to redeem us,
> Nor could He have been raised in His physical body.

Lord, I will be victorious over false teaching because
      Greater is the Holy Spirit in me, than the spirit of the world.
Those who speak the language of the world
      Get attention from the world;
      They are not from You.
But I am Your child and I know You listen to me
      And those who belong to You, listen to me;
      This is how I tell the Spirit of truth from the spirit of falsehood.

Lord, I pray Your children will love one another
      Since love comes from You, and everyone who is
      Born again has been given the gift of love.
Those who fail to love other people, have never known You
      Because You are love.
Your love for me was revealed when You sent Your Only Son
      Into the world, so that I could have life through Him.
What is love? Not that I loved You, but that You loved us
      And sent Your Son as a sacrifice to take away my sins.
Since You have loved me so much,
      I ought to love other believers.

No one has ever seen You at any time, but as long
      As I love other believers, You will live in me,
      And Your love will be seen through me.
Thank You for putting the Holy Spirit into my heart
      As a proof that You live in me, and I live in You.

Furthermore, John saw with his eyes and writes to tell us
      You sent the Son to save the world.
Those who acknowledge that Jesus is Your Son
      Lives in You, and You in them.
I know You love me deeply because I felt Your love for me;
      You are love, and whoever lives a life of love,
      Lives in You, and You live in them.
Your love will be complete in me when I stand

Perfect before the judgment seat.
There is no fear in love, because perfect love
    Drives out fear.
It is those who do not love who are fearful because they
    Do not know what will happen to them in judgment;
    That proves they are not Your children.
So, my love for You comes because You first loved me;
    Those who say, "I love God" but hate a fellow Christian
    Whom they can see; cannot love You whom they cannot see.
So this is the summary of love: anyone who loves You,
    Must also love their brother or sister.

Lord, I love You with all my heart, mind, and body;
    Keep me always in the center of Your will.

Amen

You Can Know You Are God's Child

1 John 5:1-21

Lord, I know I am born again, because I believe
    Jesus is the Messiah. And all who love You,
    Love Your children also.
I know I am Your child because I love You, and
    I do what You have commanded me to do.

This is what loving You means—keeping Your commandments
    Because they are not difficult.
I know I am Your child because I have victoriously
    Overcome the lust of the world by faith.
Who else can overcome the world? Only those who believe
    Jesus is the Son of God;
    Jesus came by water and blood,
    His blood was shed to cleanse us from sin,

And water stands for our Spirit baptism into the body.
The Holy Spirit is another witness that I am Your child;
    The Holy Spirit witnesses in me that I am born again.
These three, the blood, water, and Spirit all agree
    That I am Your child.
Many people accept a man's witness to the truth,
    But Your witness is much greater.
I know I am born again because I have Your witness within;
    Everyone who believes in Your Son has life,
    Those who reject Your Son, make You out to be a liar,
But I know I am born again because of Your testimony
    In Your Word thatYou have given us Your Son;
    Those who have the Son have eternal life;
I know I am born again because I have Your Son in my heart.
    I also have assurance because You said those who have
    The Son, have eternal life.
I also know I am born again because You hear my prayers,
    And I know You will answer my prayers because
    You do not hear and answer the prayers of unsaved people.
Lord, I will pray for those who commit a sin that
    Does not lead to death and You will give them life.
There is a fatal sin which ends in death;
    I will not pray on this occasion,
    All wrong doing is sin, but not all sin is fatal.
I know I am born again because I do not continually practice sin
    Because the Son of God protects me from the evil one.
I know I am born again because I realize all non-Christians are lost;
    Your children have this spiritual insight.
I know the Son of God has come into my heart to give me
    Spiritual understanding to know You;
    I know You are the true God who gives eternal life.
Lord, I will watch out for anything that takes Your place
    In my heart.

Lord, thank You for assurance of salvation;
  Only Your children can live a life full of confidence.

Amen

Second John

PRAYING THE BOOK OF SECOND JOHN 1–13

THE STORY OF WRITING THE SECOND LETTER OF JOHN

John called out to his valet, "Get pen, ink, and paper." Immediately, young Ansel came running into the room where the ancient apostle was waiting. John explained, "I will write immediately to the church."

Young Ansel was only gone for a few minutes, then he returned with a writing box, containing ink, several quills, and writing paper. Even though John was over 90 years of age, his mind was keen and his eyes were sharp. He could see clearly what he wanted to write. Taking the feather in hand, he squeezed the barrel, dipped it into the ink to suck the black olive oil up into the barrel of the feather. Then placing his quill on the paper, he slowly wrote out the words, "The elder unto the elect lady...."

"Sir...," young Ansel interrupted John, "why don't you write 'from the apostle,' that will give the letter more validity?"

"You mean authority like Paul?" John answered. "Do you want me to speak harshly to the church as my good friend Paul sometimes had to do?" John shook his head negatively, "I don't have to exercise my apostolic authority."

Meekly, young Ansel's head bobbed affirmatively.

John continued, "Paul had to use the word 'apostle' because some doubted if he were an apostle." Then the old man explained, "Paul never followed the Lord three and a half years through Galilee like I did. Paul never leaned his head on Jesus' breast as I did. Everyone knows I followed the Lord, so everyone knows I'm an apostle. Because Paul was saved after Jesus went back to Heaven, some doubted his apostleship. No one doubts me."

Ansel shook his head in agreement.

Then the old apostle wrote, "The elder unto the church which is an elect lady and to all the churches she planted, i.e., her children..."[1]

"I could just write from John, that's all I need. But that sounds as though I am exalting myself above the church." John shook his head negatively and thought for a moment. Again he looked down at the blank sheet of paper.

"The elder unto the...elect lady..." John wrote. "I like that, and what I have written shall remain."

Young Ansel said to John, "Who is the lady to whom you are writing?"

John put his pen back, pushed himself back in the chair, and smiled. He didn't say anything for a long time and then remarked, "The lady is the church! Don't you remember the picture of the church as a bride? I think a beautiful bride is a good picture of the church." John smiled and asked a question, "Don't you remember that the church is married to Jesus Christ?"

Ansel nodded in agreement, he did remember.

"So, I'll call the church *elect lady*, is that agreeable to you, Ansel?"

Again he nodded his head in approval.

Several times in the letter John referred to his personal observations about the church. He mentioned the phrase, "I was very glad when I found my children walking in the truth."

As John grew older, he saw more and more false teachings slipping into the church. It was the passion of the elderly John that every person worship the Lord Jesus Christ accurately. He wanted every believer to know that Jesus was fully God, yet He was fully human; he wanted everyone to know that the Word became *flesh*.

So John warned in the letter, "Many deceivers who deny the faith have spread out everywhere telling people that Jesus Christ did not come in the flesh. Anyone who says this is deceived and deceives other people. He is just as bad as the antichrist."

As a matter of fact, John was so concerned about these deceivers he said, "Anyone who doesn't abide in the doctrine of Christ, was never saved in the first place; they don't have the presence of God in their life." Then John smiled, "Those who abide in the true doctrine of Christ, they have the Father and the Son, Jesus Christ."

Endnote

1. 2 John 1:1 (ELT).

Praying the Book of Second John

Live the Truth

2 John 1–13

A letter from the elderly John,
> To the church who is an Elect Lady
And Her Children whom I love in truth:

"I and everyone in the Body of Christ love you in the faith
> Because the Word of God dwells in your heart and in ours,
Grace, mercy and peace from God the Father
> And the Lord Jesus Christ, the Son of the Father."
"I am glad that I found your children—church plants—walking in truth
> And obeying God's Word."
"Now, I urgently remind you of the Christian principle that you love
> one another; This is the commandment I wrote to you from
> the beginning
> That when we love one another, we keep His words."

Lord, give me a deeper love for the brethren and help me express it;
Help me receive love from others, and in that relationship
  May our love grow to overcome all our weaknesses.

"Watch out for false teachers who believe and teach
    That Jesus Christ was born only with a human body,
    And that He was not deity."
"These false teachers are deceivers and antichrists;
    Keep a watchful eye that you do not lose
    The prize for which you and I work."
"Be constant so you receive your full reward
    For being faithful in all things
Because if you wander from the teachings of Christ,
    You will lose God's influence in your life."
"Those who remain true to Christian doctrine,
    Have both the Father and the Son."
"If anyone comes teaching that Jesus Christ
    Is not equal in nature to the Father,
    Do not receive him or give him hospitality,
Nor recommend him to other churches
    Because those who support him,
    Will become partners in his false teaching."
"I have many things to explain, but
    I will not write them with pen and paper."
"We will both be satisfied when I come
    And speak personally with you about these things;
    The children of your 'sister' greet you."

Lord, I believe You inspired every word of the Bible,
    So it is accurate and I can rely on it to know the truth.
Keep me from using my opinions to interpret Your Word;
    I yield to the Holy Spirit to guide me to understand the Bible
    So I can accurately know and teach Your will to them.

Amen

Third John

PRAYING THE BOOK OF THIRD JOHN
1–14

THE STORY OF WRITING THE THIRD LETTER OF JOHN

The aged John's voice cracked as he called, "Ansel." John's valet came running to his side, "Diotrophes is up to his old tricks," John the apostle of love didn't feel loving today. He snarled when he spit out the words, "Diotrophes is up to his old tricks again."

The church in Ephesus had sent preachers up to a well-known church in the hills. This church body had many wonderful people in it, but Diotrophes was one of the elders in the church who somehow seized control of the pulpit, and no one could preach there without his permission. Diotrophes had gathered control of the money, and nothing was spent without Diotrophes' permission. Diotrophes had made himself boss of the church, and when the apostle John sent a preacher to the church, Diotrophes wouldn't let him preach.

"Diotrophes loves to have the preeminence," John told his young servant, Ansel. Then John added, "I like what my friend the apostle Paul said, 'That in all things, Christ shall have the preeminence.'[1]

Ansel asked John, "Why doesn't Gaius do something?" Gaius was a good friend of John's and was one of the elders in the church. Gaius had a level head about things. Gaius was a true servant of Christ and opposed all Diotrophes did in the church.

John agreed and said, "I'll write a letter to Gaius to correct the problem. When Gaius reads this letter to the church, people will understand what's going on and do something."

"How about Demetrius?" Ansel asked about another elder in the church. "Demetrius also has a good report of everyone?" the young Ansel added.

"Demetrius will support Gaius," John answered. Then added to his letter, "The two of them—Demetrius and Gaius—will stop Diotrophes."

John shook his head in disgust as he explained that Diotrophes had rejected letters from the apostles and even rejected the authority of the apostles themselves. Diotrophes acted like he was an apostle, but he never followed Christ, he never saw Christ in His resurrected body, and he sure did not act like Christ.

John told his young servant, "I shall write a letter to the church before I go there." John explained that the church body was the final seat of authority and when the people of the church don't follow Diotrophes, he would lose his authority. John wanted the church to know why he was coming and what he would do when he got there.

"Yes…that's what I'll do. I'll explain to the church that Diotrophes is wrong. If no one in the church follows him, Diotrophes will lose his power."

Endnote

1. Col. 1:18.

Praying the Book of Third John

Watch Out for Church Dictators

3 John 1–14

This letter is from the elder John
    To the well-beloved Gaius, a church leader whom I love:

"I am praying for you to prosper physically
    As you prosper spiritually."
"I rejoiced when I heard from different traveling ministers;
    They told me you are standing for the truth,

And you are living by the truth."
"Nothing could make me happier than to hear
That those I led to Christ are faithful to the Word of God."

Dear Friend, thank you for giving hospitality to the traveling
Preachers and missionaries who came through your town;
They told the church in Ephesus of your friendship and help."
"Thank you for sending them on their way with a financial gift
Because they travel for the Lord without a salary,
And they refuse to take money from the unsaved,
Even though they attended their meetings and received their ministry."
"Remember, the churches have the responsibility to care for them
financially,
Thus becoming fellow-workers with them in the truth."

Lord, thank You for those men of God who teach me the Word of God;
May I grow spiritually because of their ministry.
Use their ministry to edify the whole Body of Christ,
And supply all their temporal needs.

"I previously wrote to the church to take care of them
But Diotrephes, who loves to boss the church, refused to listen
to my advice."
"If I am able to come, I will show you the evil things
He is saying against the Ephesian church."
He refuses to allow the preachers we sent to carry out their ministry,
Nor will he allow others in the church to listen to them;
He kicks them out of the church."
"Dear Friend, do not follow his terrible example,
Pattern your life after a good example;
When the believers in your church do what is right,
They prove they are God's children."
"Everyone recognizes Demetrius does the right things,
So receive him when he delivers this letter to you;
I know he will tell you the truth and answer your questions."

"I have many things to tell you but I can't write them
    Because I hope to see you soon,
    Then we can talk about them; Peace to you."
"Friends here send their love;
    Give everyone a special greeting from me."

Lord, it's so easy to be blinded by our own self importance;
    Keep me from being egocentric and tyrannical like Diotrephes.
May I humbly see my place in the whole Body of Christ and fit in;
    May believers love to be around me because I build them up.
Lord, may I be sensitive to leaders and followers in the church;
    May I build up Your Body, not tear it apart.

Amen

Jude

PRAYING THE BOOK OF JUDE
1: 1–25

THE STORY OF THE WRITING OF THE BOOK OF JUDE

The Man With Three Names

A craggy old apostle carefully chose his steps between rounded stones climbing to a mountain village where he was to preach to a small church. They were located in a small valley way up off the main road. The Christians babbled with excitement all week because they had never had an apostle preach to them, especially a "distinguished" preacher like this who actually walked with Jesus on earth.

The apostle's thick grey-white silky smooth beard bounced with the wind as he continued climbing. The climb was difficult. His dark brown face looked like that of a workman who had spent his life in the sun. The dark face made his grey beard and white hair shine all the more.

The apostle was proud of his Hebrew name, Judah, because it meant *praise*. Why was he proud? Judah was the largest tribe in Israel, and Judah was the son of Jacob who was spokesman for the rest. And hadn't Jesus been born of the tribe of Judah? As a matter of fact, this apostle named Judah had always been proud of his distinct name and the position it gave to him. But lately he was not sure. Lately his name caused difficulties.

Judah entered the home of a wealthy businessman whose large dining room was filled with Christians. He had gotten lost on his way to the village, so he was a few minutes late. The Christians were already singing psalms when he arrived. Judah hadn't time to meet the individual believers, so he went straight to the front of the room to introduce himself. He didn't introduce himself with the Hebrew Judah, but with the Greek pronunciation, Judas.

"Good evening, my name is Judas, I am a disciple of Jesus Christ."

The room erupted in outrage. "NO ..." some men yelled out threats to crucify him. "We won't hear you." Others yelled divine curses at him, thinking he was Judas, the one who betrayed Jesus Christ. Some called him traitor and Beelzebub.

Judas shook his head and began pleaded for silence, "No, no, no, I am not Judas Iscariot who betrayed Jesus Christ." He explained when the crowd began to soften its rhetoric, "I'm the other Judas who followed Jesus. Remember, I'm the one in the upper room who said, "How can you reveal Yourself to us and not to the world?"[1]

Judas should have known better, this same experience happened at other churches when they didn't now who he was. Many had never memorized the 12 disciples' names so they didn't know there were two named Judas. Obviously, Judas Iscariot was better recognized because he was hated for betraying Jesus.

The following morning, the apostle Judas walked down the mountain from the young church, reflecting on what had happened, "What am I going to do?" Judas asked himself. He didn't want to turn every church meeting into a shouting match. And then someone told him it was dangerous because some "hot head" might react swiftly to kill him because of their hatred for Judas Iscariot.

"I'll change my name," Judas thought to himself. "I'll no longer call myself by the Greek Judas, but I'll call myself Thaddeus, because that is the Aramaic name for *Praise*. Thaddeus will remind me of my Hebrew name Judah that also means praise."

Later Thaddeus was called "Lebbaeous" which is the root word for *white*. Everyone knew him by his snow white beard and hair. He became Thaddeus, the man with the flashing white hair.

For several years Judah was called Lebbaeous Thaddeus and by that name was accepted into churches. There were no violent clashes. However, after traveling to churches for several decades he realized he had to always explain his "new" name, Lebbaeous Thaddeus.

A few places still reacted to him, thinking he was not an apostle. A few who had memorized the Jewish names of the 12 apostles didn't recognize the Gentile name, Lebbaeous Thaddeus. Then one day he thought to himself, "I'd like to go back to my original name, but I can't use the Hebrew name Judah, nor could I use the Greek name, Judas; I'll use the Latin name, Jude.

Inasmuch as he no longer was traveling the Holy Land, now he was preaching in churches filled with Romans who spoke Latin. So Jude started using the Latin name, Jude.

Two hundred years after the death of Christ, Jerome, the early church father, called Jude Trinomious, i.e., the man with three names.

Endnote

1. John 14:23.

Praying the Book of Jude

Sinful Living Leads to Doctrinal Heresy

Jude 1–25

Lord, I thank You for Jude, a servant of Jesus Christ;
    Thank You that he wrote to me and
    Grace to believers everywhere who have obeyed Your call,
    And You keep them in the faith of Jesus Christ.
May I experience Your daily presence in my daily walk with You;
    Lord, I receive Your mercy, peace, and love.
Jude had planned to write about the wonderful truths
    Of the salvation we share in common,
But he found it necessary to urge us in this letter

To be prepared to defend the complete faith
That You have once for all given to us,
Because some have infiltrated the churches
Who are the ones I have been previously warned about;
These people were condemned for denying Your truth and
Have turned Your freedom into an opportunity to sin,
As a result, they have rejected the authority of my Master, Jesus Christ.

Lord, I rejoice that You delivered Israel from the slavery of Egypt,
Even though You later destroyed those rebels who went back to sin.
I also read about the sinless angels who rebelled against You
That You threw them into hell to be chained until the day of
judgment.

Lord, help me remember that when Christians give into sexual sins
They are blinded by their lust, and they lose their understanding
of truth,
Just as Israel was rebellious of You and became blinded to heresy.
Lord, keep me sexually pure and give me strength to live right,
So I will properly know the truth, and correctly live by it.
Lord, help me remember You created angels sinless and beautiful
Yet you punished them for their sin,
Help me live a holy life.

Finally, I read about those in Sodom and Gomorrah who lusted after
sexual sin,
Including unnatural lust of men with men.
You destroyed those cities with fire as a warning to us
That there is punishment in hell for those who give themselves
to sin.

Lord, today false teachers still rebel against You
By living their sinful immoral lives, defiling their bodies,
Laughing at those in authority over them and despising Your
messengers.

Not even Michael dared to denounce the devil over the corpse of Moses
>But said, "The Lord rebuke you."

But these false teachers will mock anything they do not understand
>And like animals they do anything they feel like doing;
>By giving into their lust, their actions become fatal.

May these false teachers get what they deserve?
>May they be punished like Cain who killed his brother;
>May they get the same reward as Balaam who cursed Israel.

They have rebelled against spiritual leadership just as Korah,
>May they share his same fate of falling into hell.

They are a dangerous threat to our fellowship at the Lord's Table
>Because they come just to get a good meal.

They are like rain clouds that are blown over the farm
>That bring no rain to give life to the fields.

They are like barren fruit trees that give no fruit,
>So let's dig them up in winter like the other fruitless trees.

They are like raging waves that threaten the ship of faith,
>Also they are like shooting stars that burn out and give no light.

Lord, help me recognize false teachers
>*And separate myself from them and their influence.*
Stop their spread of evil to religious people
>*Who follow their lust, not the Word of God.*

Enoch, who lived seven generations from Adam
>Knew about these false teachers when he preached and predicted,
>"You will come with millions of Saints
>To pronounce judgment on all those who reject You
>And judge the wicked for all the wickedness they have done,
>And to punish those who speak defiantly against You."

False teachers are complainers, malcontents, doing only
>What their desires—lusts—drive them to do.

They boast and brag about their spirituality, and they give "lip service"
    To leaders in the church, but they do it to their advantage.

Lord, Jude had godly hatred for false teachers who destroy
    People with their false teaching;
    Give me a passion to be true in all I know and believe.

Lord, the Lord Jesus Christ told the apostles
    That in the last days there would be scoffers
    Who will live according to their sinful lust.
These false teachers will split churches, stir up arguments;
    They do not have the Holy Spirit to teach them truth
    Or to convict them of their evil imagination and sin.

Lord, I commit myself to becoming strong in your faith;
    I will pray in the power of the Holy Spirit.
I will keep myself within the constraints of Your love
    And wait patiently for Jesus Christ to give me eternal life.
I will have mercy on those who have doubts,
    And I will try to help those who argue against you.
I will point them to You by being kind to them;
    Some You will save by snatching them from the flaming hell,
    I will be careful I'm not pulled into their sin and into hell itself.
I will hate everything about their sin,
    Being careful not to be contaminated by their lust.

Lord, even though Jude hated false teaching, he had compassion
    On those believers who were deceived by false teachers;
    Give me that same compassion to help uneducated believers.

Now I praise You because You can keep me from falling,
    And You can deliver me faultless into Your glorious presence
    So that I am happy and preserved in Christ.
To You, the only God who saves me through our Lord Jesus Christ,

To You be glory, majesty, authority, and power
In the ages past, now, and forever in the future.

Lord, Jude probably hated false teachers because he was
Mistaken for Judas Iscariot. No wonder he hated false teachers so
deeply.
Keep me close to Your truth all my life.

Amen

ABOUT THE AUTHOR

D r. Elmer Towns is an author of popular and scholarly works, a seminar lecturer, and dedicated worker in Sunday school. He has written over 125 books, including several best sellers. In 1995 he won the coveted Gold Medallion Book Award for *The Names of the Holy Spirit*.

Dr. Elmer Towns also cofounded Liberty University with Jerry Falwell in 1971 and now serves as Dean of the B.R. Lakin School of Religion and as professor of Theology and New Testament.

Liberty University was founded in 1971 and is the fastest growing Christian university in America. Located in Lynchburg, Virginia, Liberty University is a private, coeducational, undergraduate and graduate institution offering 38 undergraduate and 15 graduate programs serving over 30,000 resident and external students (11,600 on campus). Individuals from all 50 states and more than 70 nations comprise the diverse student body. While the faculty and students vary greatly, the common denominator and driving force of Liberty University since its conception is love for Jesus Christ and the desire to make Him known to the entire world.

For more information about Liberty University, contact:

Liberty University
1971 University Boulevard
Lynchburg, VA 24502
Telephone 434-582-2000
E-mail: www.Liberty.edu

Dr. Towns's E-mail: www.eltowns@liberty.edu.
Type in "My Book Store" to order Dr. Towns's books.

ALSO FROM ELMER TOWNS

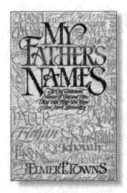

My Father's Names
The Old Testament Names of God
and How They Can Help You
Know Him More Intimately
Elmer L. Towns
ISBN 08307.14472

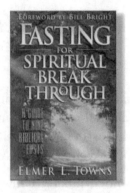

**Fasting for Spiritual
Breakthrough**
A Guide to Nine Biblical Fasts
Elmer L. Towns
ISBN 08307.18397
Study Guide • ISBN 08307.18478

How to Pray
When You Don't Know What to Say
Elmer L. Towns
ISBN 08307.41879

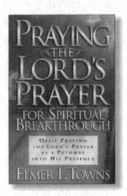

**Praying the Lord's Prayer
for Spiritual Breakthrough**
Elmer L. Towns
ISBN 08307.20421
Video • Approximately 160 min.
UPC 607135.002901

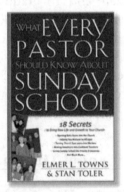

**What Every Pastor Should
Know About Sunday
School**
18 Secrets to Bring New Life and
Growth to Your Church
Elmer L. Towns
ISBN 08307.28597

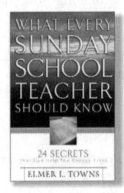

**What Every Sunday School
Teacher Should Know**
24 Secrets that Can Help
You Change Lives
Elmer L. Towns
ISBN 08307.28740
Video • Approximately 120 min.
UPC 607135.006091

Praying the Psalms
To Touch God and
Be Touched by Him
Elmer Towns
ISBN: 0-7684-2195-0

Praying the Proverbs
Including Ecclesiastes and
the Song of Solomon
Elmer Towns
ISBN: 0-7684-2316-3

Praying the Book of Job
Learning How to Endure
Life's Hardships
Elmer Towns
ISBN: 0-7684-2361-9

**Knowing God
Through Fasting**
Foreword by Tommy Tenney
Elmer Towns
ISBN: 0-7684-2069-5

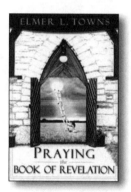

**Praying the Book
of Revelation**
Elmer Towns
ISBN: 0-7684-2420-8

Praying the Gospels
Matthew, Mark, Luke and John
Elmer Towns
ISBN: 0-7684-2439-9

Personal Revelation